101

AMAZING THINGS

about DOG LOVERS

Todd & Jedd Hafer

BroadStreet
PUBLISHING

BroadStreet Publishing Group, LLC
Racine, Wisconsin, USA
BroadStreetPublishing.com

IOI AMAZING THINGS ABOUT DOG LOVERS

ISBN-13: 978-1-4245-5386-0 (hardcover)
ISBN-13: 978-1-4245-5387-7 (e-book)

Cover design by Chris Garborg, GarborgDesign.com
Typesetting by Katherine Lloyd, theDESKonline.com

Printed in China

17 18 19 20 21 5 4 3 2 1

Contents

Introduction

Dogs. They descended from the wild and mighty wolf and first crossed paths with us thousands of years ago. Early in humans' relationship with them, dogs lived on the fringes of villages or encampments, but it wasn't long before canines were welcomed into the heart of civilization—and into the hearts of women, men, and children. For example, a grave from ancient Israel held the skeletons of an old man and the puppy he cradled in his arms.

Thousands of years before the birth of Christ, dogs assisted people on hunts, joined them in battle, carried their goods, and sat with them by the fire. The Talmud extols dogs as faithful companions and protectors, noting that God gave Cain, though he was a sinner, a dog as a symbol of His mercy and divine protection. Some Christians believe that the shepherds who visited the baby Jesus brought dogs with them, which is why some nativity scenes include dogs. And according to legend, Saint Patrick was guided by a large gray dog whose chest bore the mark of a white cross.

Today, we love our dogs for myriad reasons. They are loving, hilarious, playful, and loyal. They accept us, quirks and all, and hope we will do the same for them. They connect with us emotionally, often without making a sound. Maybe that is why almost half of all dogs sleep with their owners. And 87 percent of our canines watch TV with us.

Within this book's covers, you'll discover truly amazing facts about dogs and the people who love them. Which U.S. president is the number-one dog fan of all? (And which president's dog once attacked a French ambassador?) Why should dogs enjoy catnip just as much as cats? Which canine actor was robbed of an Academy Award? And why should we thank dogs for advances in cancer detection?

There are at least 101 intriguing things to discover about America's most loyal pet. So kick back with your dog and let some remarkable canines and their "people" walk their way into your heart.

Who knows—maybe you'll find yourself loving your dog (or dogs) more. If that's even possible.

> "We dogs were once wild and cunning. We had sharp instincts and the eyes of predators. And then we learned you had soft beds and comfy pillows."
> *Jedd Hafer*

> "Dogs just need you and love. That's all."
> *Jennifer Westfeldt*

GREAT MINDS THINK ALIKE?

In this book, you'll read a lot about the friendly—well, mostly friendly—rivalry between dog lovers and cat lovers. (And it's wonderful that lots of people are both!)

Those in the dog camp like to point out that cats' brains are relatively small, composing just 0.9 percent of their body mass. But, according to *Psychology Today* magazine, "The brains of cats have an amazing surface folding and a structure that is about 90 percent similar to ours [humans']." Further, the cerebral cortex, the brain region responsible for processing information, is more complex in cats than in dogs. A cat's brain boasts 300 million neurons. A dog's? Only 160 million.

But that neuron disparity doesn't seem to account for the fact that dogs can be taught a variety of tricks and activities—from the simple "Sit" and "Stay" to finding the TV remote, putting toys away, and even "Stop, Drop, and Roll." Further, in a 2002 Harvard University study, dogs outperformed even super-smart chimpanzees in various tests of cognitive acumen. One test gauged the participants' ability to decipher signals from humans who were indicating the location of hidden food. Dogs easily outperformed a group of trained chimps when it came to understanding human cues.

Of course, cats can ace tests too. In a 2010 experiment, a sophisticated super-computer performed *eighty-three times slower* than a cat's brain!

So, it seems that in the "Who's Smarter?" battle, both the dog people and the cat people have plenty of ammo. Both kinds of pets have amazing minds that should be respected. It's the smart thing to do.

Speaking of Dogs . . .

"A well-trained dog is like religion. It sets the deserving at their ease and is a terror to evildoers."

Elizabeth Goudge

Do not be wise in your own eyes;
fear the LORD and shun evil.

PROVERBS 3:7

2

"TOTO, I'VE GOT A FEELING WE'RE NOT IN KANSAS ANYMORE."

The term *trending* wasn't in vogue in 1939, but had it been, it would have been applied to a small dog with a huge role in one of the most celebrated movies of all time.

Terry, a Cairn terrier, was a mere pup when she was adopted by dog trainer Carl Spitz after being rejected by her owner. Spitz began working with his new pupil, and in just a few months landed Terry in the 1934 movie *Bright Eyes*, starring alongside Shirley Temple. (Early in Terry's screen test with the child star, Temple turned to the adults nearby and informed them, "She's hired.")

Terry starred in five more films before auditioning for 1939's *The Wizard of Oz*. The little five-year-old Cairn out-acted more than one hundred other dogs and landed the role of Toto. Terry was paid $125 a week for her role, more than many of the movie's human actors. If this seems unfair, watch the movie and note how many scenes include or feature Toto. In fact, the role was so popular that, according to some estimates, 30 percent of all small-breed dogs born in the year after the film were named Toto. This number includes Terry herself, because so many people referred to his Terry as "Toto" that Carl Spitz changed the dog's name to appease everyone.

Toto/Terry went on to star in a total of thirteen films. She died in 1945 at age eleven and was buried at Spitz's ranch in Studio City, California.

Incidentally, some scholars have argued over the deeper, metaphysical meaning of Toto. One theory is that Toto represents Anubis, the dog-headed Egyptian god of death, because it was Toto who consistently hampered Dorothy's efforts to return home. This theory might not hold any validity, but it does show what can happen when scholars have too much time to ponder.

For the real story on Toto, you can read *I Toto: The Autobiography of Terry, the Dog Who Was Toto*. Toto's human collaborator for this first-person saga was Willard Carroll, co-founder of the Oz Museum.

Speaking of Dogs . . .

"I think dogs are the most amazing creatures;
they give unconditional love. For me, they are
the role model for being alive."

Gilda Radner

From generation to generation
we will proclaim your praise.

PSALM 79:13

3

A NEW TRICK FOR OLD DOGS

If you have an older dog, you might think he is just slowing down because of age. Do any of the following statements sound familiar?

1. My dog's gait seems stiff and slow.
2. My dog is starting to walk with a slight limp and seems sore when patted or rubbed.
3. My dog lags behind me on walks.
4. My dog is behaving out of character—acting aggressively or withdrawn without any obvious explanation.
5. My dog is struggling to get in the car or climb up on a favorite resting place.

Even longtime dog people can misinterpret the signs of canine osteoarthritis as one of the inevitable signs of old age. Osteoarthritis (OA) is a degenerative joint disease brought on by deterioration of cartilage surrounding the joints. It causes chronic joint inflammation and is the most common cause of lameness in dogs, affecting one in five dogs, with older canines bearing the highest risk.

Fortunately, savvy dog lovers are taking advantage of revolutionary new treatments, including two that are drug-free and derived from a dog's own cells. A treatment called ReGen OA is a stem-cell treatment with the dog as both donor and recipient. It addresses OA symptoms and repairs damaged tissues. A similar treatment, called EvolGen OA, is a plasma-based approach that targets pain and inflammation and slows the progress of joint degeneration.

For more information about these or other leading-edge treatments (which are safe but not inexpensive), consult your veterinarian.

Speaking of Dogs . . .

"Blessed is the person who has earned
the love of an old dog."
Sidney Jeanne Seward

For you have delivered … my feet from stumbling,
that I may walk before God in the light of life.

PSALM 56:13

4

DOMESTIC DINGOES?

Many people view wild animals like wolves, foxes, and dingoes as forebears of the domesticated dog. In the case of the dingo, that is probably an incorrect assumption.

The dingo is, most likely, a domestic dog that *became* wild. DNA studies have shown that dingoes are closely related to domestic dogs in East Asia. Scientists believe that Chinese explorers were often accompanied by dogs, who provided both companionship and protection and (sadly) served as food. About 3,500 years ago, some of these dogs journeyed to Australia, where they bred and became the dingoes we know today.

Dingoes eat a varied carnivore diet, including everything from lizards to rodents to kangaroos. In an interesting twist in the saga of this animal, some dingoes have been tamed (re-tamed?) and today are kept as pets by the Aboriginal people in Australia.

Speaking of Dogs . . .

"Dogs are the only animals who will answer to their names and recognize the voices of the family. Next to man, there is no living creatures whose memory is so retentive."

Pliny the Elder, circa 78 CE

Spread your protection over them,
that those who love your name may rejoice in you.

PSALM 5:11

Most Popular Dogs in the United States

(according to American Kennel Association registration statistics)

1. Labrador retriever

2. German shepherd

3. Golden retriever

4. Bulldog

5. Beagle

6. Yorkshire terrier

7. Poodle

8. Boxer

9. French bulldog

10. Rottweiler

A DOG UP YOUR SLEEVE

Today's purse and handbag dogs have nothing on the dogs of ancient Asia.

In China, circa 1000 BCE, the royalty bred small dogs, called sleeve dogs, as cherished companions. These dogs were small enough to fit into the flowing sleeve of a nobleman. Later, Buddhists in Asia began to breed small dogs that resembled lions. (According to legend, lions were fiercely loyal to Buddha.) These "lion dogs" or "Fo Dogs" were believed to be actual lions—but with the appearance and submissiveness of a pet dog.

Before long, the Fo Dog was embraced (figuratively and literally) in India, China, Tibet, Japan, and Korea. Many varieties of the tiny lion dogs were bred, including the Pekingese, Lhasa Apso, Tibetan terrier, and the Shih Tzu. These dogs were beloved as status symbols and companions, as well as for their religious significance.

Today's dogs might not have as much religious significance as their ancestors, but many dog people still regard their four-legged friends with a devotion that borders on worship. This, of course, is fine with the canines.

Did You Know?

Dogs were portrayed on coins in both ancient Rome and ancient Greece.

᏶

"Who dares despise the day of small things?"

ZECHARIAH 4:10

BARKING UP THE WRONG TREE?

Habitual barking is a challenge for many dog owners. Theories abound on why dogs bark, and many of them are supported by actual evidence. Dogs bark for many reasons, which is why barking is often a behavioral problem that needs to be addressed.

One reason dogs bark is that they don't get enough exercise. An under-exercised dog barks a lot because it gives her some of the physical activity that's missing from her daily routine. A healthy young dog needs at least an hour of vigorous running or playing every day. Without this exercise, the dog can become antsy, barking at everything that moves, just for something to do.

So if you have a habitual barker at home (*canine* barker only), try upping the activity level. Take long walks, particularly on hilly routes. Play fetch or tug-of-war. And if your schedule or other factors prevent you from providing daily dog exercise, consider doggy daycare, which often includes indoor and/or outdoor play. You could also hire a dog walker or find a neighbor or friend who might help out for a small fee, in exchange for a favor, or simply to be a Good Samaritan.

Of course, even a well-exercised dog can have a barking problem. Some dogs bark out of boredom; it gives them something interesting to do with their mouths. If this sounds like your dog, try a food-dispensing toy. These toys come in a variety of shapes, sizes, and textures, and the right one can keep a dog engaged (and bark-free) for a long time.

If you have an indoor dog who loves to bark at various beings, vehicles, and other outside entities, try obscuring the view of all that bark-inducing stimuli. Savvy pet owners rearrange furniture, put up opaque fencing, or strategically plant foliage to obscure various bark-tempters, such as passing cars or strolling neighbors.

Here's one solution that smart dog people avoid: adopting a second dog to quiet a barker. This dog duet usually increases the total noise factor, since two dogs together typically bark more than twice as much as a single pooch. Call it bark synergy.

Did You Know?

Many dog owners have found citronella anti-bark collars to be an effective deterrent. These collars emit a burst of pungent but harmless citronella when a dog barks, and the smell startles and distracts the dog. However, a clever canine quickly learns the following: "If I bark nonstop for the next fifteen minutes or so, I can empty the reservoir of this strange-smelling stuff. Then I can bark all I want without triggering anymore stinky bursts."

🕶

When he opened the seventh seal,
there was silence in heaven for about half an hour.

REVELATION 8:1

7

A DOG IS A CLASS ACT

In the late 1920s, the biggest star in Hollywood had great legs. Four of them.

Rin Tin Tin (also known as Rinty) was a German shepherd rescued from a French battlefield during World War I by American soldier Lee Duncan. After the war, Duncan trained Rinty and managed to get him small roles in a few silent films. Soon, Rinty was a top dog in Hollywood. He starred in four hit movies in 1927 alone, and in one poll, he was voted Most Popular Performer in America. He signed all of his contracts with a paw print.

In 1929, Rinty starred in *Where the North Begins*. That role led to a nomination for the Best Actor Academy Award. In fact, Hollywood legend has it that Rinty actually received the most votes. However, the Academy ultimately decided that the award should to go a human. This was a huge relief to bi-pedal performer Emil Jannings, who got the Best Actor nod.

Nonetheless, *Where the North Begins* was a smash success. In fact, Rinty is often credited for rescuing Warner Brothers Studios from the brink of bankruptcy. All told, Rinty starred in twenty-eight films, and he sparked a huge interest in German shepherds as pets. At the height of his popularity, the canine star received more than ten thousand fan letters a week.

However, like many Silver Screen stars, Rinty evoked his share of controversy. Decades after Rinty's near-Oscar, Warner brother Jack confessed that his studio had bred eighteen Rin Tin Tin look-alikes who appeared in many of the films. The reason?

The original Rinty, according to Warner, was an ill-tempered actor who was difficult to work with.

Did You Know?

The original Rin Tin Tin died in the arms of actress Jean Harlow. Harlow lived across the street from Rinty and reportedly sprinted to his side when she heard that the beloved neighborhood dog was ill.

I find rest in God; only he can save me.

PSALM 62:1 NCV

8

THE CANINE TIMELINE

How long have dogs, as we know them, been around? Scientists' answers differ. Some say the dog diverged from a wolf (or a wolf-like ancestor). Others argue that dogs came into being about 15,000 years ago. The Bible says God created land animals on the sixth day of creation. Whatever the case, dogs didn't become like the canines we know today until their lives intersected with ours.

Canines were first attracted to human settlements for the scavenging opportunities. They found these settlements to be a buffet of food scraps and other edible refuse. (We could be specific about this refuse, but we won't. And you should thank us.)

Over time, people grew used to these scroungers. We appreciated the free clean-up service, which kept rodents and other undesirable critters away. Also, as the scavenging dogs became territorial over their refuse heaps, they barked and growled at approaching strangers, human or otherwise. The settlers valued this free alarm service too.

Once the dogs began to receive names—and new puppies were presented as gifts to village children—the bond between people and their pet dogs was sealed.

Thousands of years have only made that bond stronger.

Did You Know?

Here are a few names of dogs owned by ancient Egyptians: Good Herdsman, Blackie, One Who Is Fashioned as an Arrow (Arrow for short), She of the Town, and Useless. Words like Bow-wow and Howler often preceded or followed each name (for example, Useless Howler or Blackie Bow-wow.)

6ㆆ

"When you enter that home,
say 'Peace be with you.'"

MATTHEW 10:12 NCV

9

SETTLING ON A SITTER

It's one of a dog lover's most daunting tasks—choosing a dog sitter. For some of us, the process is as rigorous as choosing a babysitter or daycare provider for our children.

To help make this process as productive as possible, here are a few questions to ask of potential canine care providers:

1. Do you have a proper business license if required by our city or state?
2. Do you know pet first aid, including CPR?
3. Are you insured and bonded?
4. Can you provide references?
5. Are you trained or certified by an organization like Pet Sitters International?
6. Do you provide a contract or service agreement that all interested parties can sign?

If you're looking for someone to watch your pet, you can download a free interview checklist and find local professional pet sitters at PetSit.com.

Did You Know?

Like dogs, cats can be trained to walk on a leash. However, you should never use a dog collar for your cat. Its neck and spinal anatomy differ from a dog's, requiring a cat-specific apparatus. Likewise, one should never use a cat leash on a small dog.

A man's wisdom illumines him
and causes his stern face to beam.

ECCLESIASTES 8:1 NASB

10

FOOD FOR THOUGHT ... AND HEALING

When Matt Koss's dog, Luna, began showing signs of kidney failure, he quickly turned to local veterinarians. Sadly, all of them gave the same bleak prognosis: There was no cure for Luna's condition. And because the kidneys regulate blood pressure and the production of red blood cells, Luna's condition was critical.

Koss respected the medical professionals, but his gut told him not to give up. He visited yet another vet, a holistic vet, who noted that supermarket-style dog foods, with their kibble-and-corn base, had been shown to cause illness. Further research and reading led Koss to conclude that a dog's diet should feature the specific foods that canines ate as they evolved over millions of years. Because dogs in the wild are both hunters and scavengers, some vets were recommending a diet regimen of animal protein and whole plant foods. Australian vet Ian Billinghurst calls it BARF (Biologically Appropriate Raw Food).

A chef by trade, Koss decided to overhaul the ailing Luna's diet. He chucked the kibble and created a diet of human-grade raw meat and bones and a variety of high-quality whole plants. Luna gobbled down the new fare, and her health took a turn for the better. Her energy returned, and she demonstrated an overall sense of improved wellness.

Koss continued to refine his recipes. He often stayed up until the early morning hours formulating new meals. Soon, he approached a local retailer about selling his dog food (and his cat food too). Before long, Primal Pet Foods was born. Customer comments poured in—reports of dogs and cats with better health, stronger teeth, lusher coats, and more positive demeanors. It was time to say goodbye to his chef job. "Hearing about what my foods were doing for pets was fuel for me," Koss explains. "It kept pumping my engine, and I didn't look back."

Today, Primal offers a full line of meals and supplements. Their meat is 100 percent human grade and free of antibiotics and steroids. In deference to the days of canine foraging, the food contains fruits and vegetables but no processed grains. "Most animals go berserk over 'feeding raw,'" Koss says. "When they hear the fridge open, they do twists and turns, and you can see how happy they are."[*]

Did You Know?
The first commercial canine food was a dog biscuit introduced in England in the early 1860s.

---

[*]   Matt Koss, *Modern Dog* magazine, moderndog.com.

⚭

The LORD is my strength and my shield;
my heart trusts in Him, and I am helped;
Therefore my heart exults, and with my song
I shall thank Him.

PSALM 28:7 NASB

11

A CO-STAR AND A FRIEND

can't imagine my life without him," actress Amanda Seyfried says of Finn.

Finn is not Seyfried's agent, favorite director, or husband. Finn is her Australian shepherd, whom she met through a production coordinator on one of her projects. Today, Seyfried takes Finn to work whenever she can. "He's in my contract for every acting job—to be allowed on U.S. sets," she told *USA Today*. (She calls herself Finn's "stage mother.") When Finn can't join Seyfried, the two Facetime regularly. The actress also requests twice-daily videos from her dog sitter.

Recently, Finn got the chance to co-star with his person in a 1980s-themed video for the Strut Your Mutt/#9000StepsChallenge. The challenge urges animal owners to walk nine thousand steps with their pets on the ninth day of each month. Seyfried and Finn walked their nine thousand steps wearing matching headbands.

This challenge is about more than just exercise; it's also to raise awareness of the more than nine thousand dogs and cats who are euthanized in shelters every day because there is simply not enough room for them.

Because Seyfried is an ambassador for the welfare organization Best Friends Animal Society, we can look for more Seyfried/Finn videos in the future.

Speaking of Dogs . . .

"Dogs are my favorite people."
Richard Dean Anderson

Therefore, as God's chosen people, holy and dearly loved,
clothe yourselves with compassion, kindness, humility,
gentleness and patience.

COLOSSIANS 3:12

12

ORIGINS OF THE ITALIAN GREYHOUND

Which of today's dog breeds is the most ancient? We may never know for sure, but we can count the diminutive Italian greyhound (I.G.) among the contenders. Skeletal remains from archeological digs in Turkey and Greece suggest that the breed is at least two thousand years old—and, obviously, *not* Italian. Drawings from Egyptian tombs point to even more ancient origins for the I.G., a breed that stands about thirteen inches at the withers and weighs about a dozen pounds.

The playful and loving I.G. was bred for hunting small game, as well as for companionship. The breed was a favorite subject of painters during the Middle Ages, and eventually this affectionate dog won its way into the hearts—and onto the laps—of kings, queens, and other members of high society, particularly in Italy during the Renaissance. From this period on, the affectionate "Velcro dog" was known as the Italian greyhound.

The breed made its way to England in the early 1600s, challenging the King Charles spaniel and the Maltese as the most popular among the nobility. The Italian greyhound was officially recognized by the American Kennel Club in 1886 and made its first appearance at the Westminster Kennel Club Dog Show in 1887. The I.G., a member of the Toy Group, has yet to win Best in Show, but when it comes to being affectionate and playful, it's always a prize winner.

Did You Know?

The Italian greyhound has a sighthound genetic makeup, meaning it will chase moving objects. For this reason, the I.G. and other sighthound animals should be kept on-leash when out of doors, or kept in a properly fenced yard or dog park.

6ꝋ

Let them give thanks to the LORD for his unfailing love and his wonderful deeds for mankind.

PSALM 107:31

13

THE BIG (?) PROBLEM
WITH PET—FRIENDLY APARTMENTS

As any dog lover who's ever tried to find a new rental abode knows, *pet friendly* is a relative term. For example, many landlords operate by the theory that small dogs cause less damage than large ones. Thus, they are more "friendly" toward a Chihuahua than a Great Dane.

So, what do you do when your large dog seems to be a large obstacle to your securing an apartment or other rental property—or checking into a hotel room after a long day of driving? Here are a few tips:

1. Present yourself as a responsible tenant or guest. Dress nicely and be upbeat. Don't whine about the policy or disparage small dogs. Instead, calmly explain how your dog is well behaved and under your control. Further, note that your dog gets along well with people and fellow pets.
2. Respond to every "No!" with a "What if …"
3. Invite the landlord or property manager to inspect your apartment or room. You can even add the stipulation to a rental agreement. Agree to pay for any damage and offer to pay a higher security deposit.
4. Offer to introduce your canine to the proprietor.

In short, don't be passive or defensive, but don't be rude or pushy either. With a reasoned approach, you might transform a large-dog "brick wall" into a small hurdle.

Speaking of Dogs . . .

"We have a mastiff, and my husband and
I have found a great system for poop-scooping our yard:
Neither one of us does it."

Constance Rivers

Each of you must bring a gift in proportion
to the way the LORD your God has blessed you.

DEUTERONOMY 16:17

14

BEING SMART ABOUT
SMARTPHONE DOG WALKING

We all know about the dangers of distracted driving—driving while texting or navigating with one hand on the wheel and the other cradling a smartphone to the ear. But the same principles apply when walking the dog. How many times have you seen someone texting or yakking while his or her dog slips its collar or tangles the leash around a street sign—or someone's leg?

Taking your dog for a walk shouldn't be an excuse to catch up on your talking or texting. Such multitasking is unfair to your dog and to everyone you encounter. Distracted dog walkers leave poop behind, cause trips and falls, and even risk their canines' lives. (If you've seen a dog escape from a distracted owner and sprint toward a busy street, you know what we mean.)

So, make dog-walking time something special for you and your dog(s). And set a good example for others in the process. It's the smart thing to do.

Did You Know?
More than a third of dog owners talk to their pets on the phone or leave voicemails for them.

👓

There is a time for everything: …
a time to be silent and a time to speak.

ECCLESIASTES 3:1, 7

A WALK ON THE WILD SIDE?

The Internet is full of people and their exotic canine or feline pets, such as a wolf or coyote, cheetah or fox. These relationships may look like adventures, but in almost all cases it's better to keep wild dogs and cats *wild*. Tigers and lions, and even smaller wildcats like bobcats and ocelots, are dangerous and unpredictable. The same is true of dingoes, foxes, wolves, and wolf-dog hybrids. Indeed, many wolf experts say that wolf dogs are unpredictable and dangerous. Further, even wolves who were raised and bottle-fed by people have behaved unpredictably. They are never truly (or completely) tamed.

For every intriguing YouTube video of a wild pet, there is a horror story, such as the Pennsylvania woman who died after being mauled by her pack of nine wolf dogs, which she had raised. (It should be noted that many states, including Pennsylvania, require people to have a license to own, breed, or sell wolf-dog hybrids, and the victim in this case was not licensed.) Another news story includes a Texas woman whose mountain lion mauled her young nephew.

Beyond these obvious drawbacks, consider that lions and tigers eat about forty pounds of meat a day, sometimes downing one hundred pounds in a single meal. A lion's weekly food bill can easily approach $400. Even the much smaller wolf can require up to fourteen pounds of meat a day, and sometimes even more.

For those who realize they cannot afford their exotic pet, the local zoo will probably not take it. Sadly, most exotic pets end up being euthanized.

Bottom line: Only qualified and well-trained (and rich) professionals should keep wild animals.

Did You Know?

An adult wolf can eat more than twenty-two pounds of meat in a single meal. That's what you call wolfing down your dinner!

ৰৈ

"Is there anyone here who, planning to build a new house, doesn't first sit down and figure the cost so you'll know if you can complete it?"

LUKE 14:28 MSG

16

A MOVING EXPERIENCE

Moving can be a stressful experience, from coordinating leases to packing boxes to forwarding mail. However, while your dog doesn't have to worry about packing the fine china or writing a check to the movers, he feels the stress too.

Why? Dogs love routine. For our four-legged family members, familiarity equals security. So when a move takes a bite out of that routine, dogs respond by chewing on the couch, whining in the corner, or relieving themselves on the carpet you just steam cleaned. Whatever the behavior, remember that your dog isn't working against you. He or she is just stressed, probably because *your* stress is contagious.

Whether your next move is cross-town or cross-country, here are a few ways to protect your pet and help all parties survive a change of address:

1. Keep to the dog's routine as much as possible, especially with meal times, potty breaks, and walks/play times. Since changes in routine throw a dog off-kilter, stick to the schedule as much as you can.

2. During the actual move, keep your pet out of the action. A stressed dog is a clingy dog—and a clingy dog doesn't make for a smooth move. Perhaps a good friend can dog sit for a day or two. Or, if you have a boarder your dog is comfortable with, this can be a

good option. (If someone dog sits for you, make sure he or she follows the routine as stated in #1 above.)

3. When you get to your new place, unpack your dog's bed, crate, and favorite toys immediately. These items will help a dog feel more relaxed, as they are familiar and smell like "home."

4. Take care of yourself. During times of stress, you are your dog's best remedy. By getting enough sleep, eating healthy, and being positive, you will set the tone for your canine friend(s).

Speaking of Dogs . . .

"Even a bad day at home with my
dog beats a good day at the office."

T. J. Hafer

6ə

God's angel sets up a circle of protection
around us while we pray.
Psalm 34:7 MSG

TO PROTECT AND SERVE

Nick Bailey served two tours of duty in Iraq. During his second tour, he was injured by a mortar. He returned to the United States suffering from post-traumatic stress disorder (PTSD) and mobility issues. While he wanted to have his German shepherd, Abel, trained as a service animal, the cost was daunting.

Enter eight-year-old Rachel Mennet, who heard of Bailey's struggle and wanted to help him. She contacted Peter and Lori Nebel, owners of a Pet Supplies Plus store in Summerville, South Carolina (and proud parents to two rescue dogs), and the Nebels let young Rachel operate a lemonade stand in their store. One glass of lemonade at a time, Rachel raised more than $6,000 for a grateful veteran—and Abel was able to begin his training.

Speaking of Dogs . . .

"I have found that when you are deeply troubled,
there are things you get from the silent devoted
companionship of a dog that you can get from
no other source."

Doris Day

👓

Serve one another humbly in love.

GALATIANS 5:13

BEFORE YOU KISS YOUR DOG …

Americans love their dogs—all seventy million-plus of them. However, among the many ways to show your canine affection, smooching her is not the best idea. Don't believe the adage that a dog's or cat's mouth is cleaner than a human's. Yes, the average human mouth harbors about 37 types of bacteria, but a dog's has 53 and a cat's has 130!

A dog's mouth can harbor a host of disease-causing bacteria, such as Pasturella, streptococcus, and staphylococcus. This shouldn't be surprising; after all, a dog is much more likely than a person to eat things like garbage and rotten food. Further, an estimated sixty million dogs develop gum disease by age three.

So, the next time you want to show your dog some love, try a cuddle, a tummy rub, or a few tender pats on the head.

To be fair, however, consider this list of things that probably harbor more germs than your dog's mouth:

1. Your kitchen sponge
2. The bottom of your purse (or gym bag)
3. Your paper currency
4. Your phone
5. The handrails in your home
6. Your TV remote (and especially the one at hotels)
7. The bedcovers at hotels

Did You Know?

Even though dogs' mouths are not cleaner than humans', a human bite is more dangerous than a dog bite. Why? The bacteria in a human mouth are more likely to cause disease than those in a dog's mouth. Of course, it's best to avoid being bitten by either species!

The mouths of the righteous utter wisdom.

PSALM 37:30

19

PET ALLERGIES: NOTHING TO SNEEZE AT

Do you suffer from allergies? If so, you're not alone. One in five Americans does. And of this sneezing, itching, and red-eyed group (which includes this book's authors), 30 percent are allergic to dogs, cats, and/or other pets.

If you have pet allergies, you probably know that it's not just a dog's hair that carries allergens. These microscopic sources of discomfort also lurk in pet saliva, dander (often from dead skin), and urine. Thus, even a hairless or so-called wire-coated dog can be an allergy source.

The "hypoallergenic" breeds, such as bichons frises and Portuguese water dogs, have a slower shed rate than other dogs.

Because they shed less, they tend to trigger fewer allergy problems. For many people, the necessary more frequent grooming (which is also more expensive due to the longer coats) is a fair trade-off for an allergy-free house.

All of this said, it's vital to remember that dogs and people are individuals. Even within a given breed, some dogs produce more allergens than others. Further, some allergies develop over time. The Portuguese water dog you got as a pup might make you weep (and not in a poignant way) when it is an adult.

Fortunately, there are myriad ways for a Sneezy and a Snoopy to co-exist. Solutions include allergy shots, dog-free zones in a home (for example, the bedroom), over-the-counter antihistamines, central air purifiers, and frequent vacuuming (with a HEPA-filtered machine). Some of these solutions have the added benefit of making a home cleaner and more sanitary.

Ask your vet and/or family doctor for more ideas.

Did You Know?

Your local veterinarian, dog groomer, and pet supply store employees are excellent sources of valuable information— beyond their obvious areas of expertise. These folks can help you find a dog walker or pet sitter. They can inform you about local leash laws. And if you are looking for an apartment or rental home, they often know the perfect pet-friendly place for you.

66

Create in me a pure heart, O God,
and renew a steadfast spirit within me.

PSALM 51:10

20

A DOGGIE CHILL PILL?

If you own an active-breed dog like a Labrador retriever, Dalmatian, Gordon setter, or Jack Russell terrier, you know that they are boundless (and bounding) bundles of energy. This is a great trait when playing chase in the backyard—but not so much when Grandma comes to visit and does not wish to be treated like a piece of playground equipment.

Fortunately, savvy owners can successfully channel and dial down that excessive energy. For starters, give your dog daily exercise appropriate to its age, breed, and physical condition. You can also provide mental and physical stimulation with treat toys, puzzle toys, and the challenge of learning new tricks.

Another option is to teach your dog to go from crazy to chilled-out with a simple training exercise. Grab a tug toy and start a low-key game of tug-of-war. After a few seconds, freeze in place, taking special care to avoid moving your hands. Don't say a word. Then, after your dog has all four paws on the floor (sitting or standing), say "Good!" and resume the game.

Repeat this step a few times to make sure the lesson is sinking in. Then it's time to add a verbal cue. The next time you stop tugging, calmly say, "Chill." Repeat this exercise a few times as well. Once your dog understands the essence of "Chill," you can apply it to other games or situations. For example, when your canine is pogo-ing maniacally because you have just walked in the door after a long day at work, stand still and calmly say, "Chill." Wait for the pup to calm down before rewarding him or her with your attention.

With some patience and persistence from you, your dog can go from Hyper Hound to Champion of Chill.

Speaking of Dogs . . .

"I am called a dog because I fawn on those who give me anything, I yelp at those who refuse, and I set my teeth in rascals."

Diogenes, 412–323 BCE

6∂

You will keep in perfect peace those whose minds are steadfast, because they trust in you.

ISAIAH 26:3

21

CATS AND DOGS: A COMMON ANCESTRY?

Dog lovers and cat lovers enjoy debating which pet is superior, and some are quick to point out the stark differences between canines and felines. However, it is possible that cats and dogs are related—as members of the same genetic household.

Some scientists say that cats and dogs both descended from a prehistoric mammal called the Miacis. Later, dogs evolved into a new species called Cynodictis.

Incidentally, canids (members of the dog family including wolves, coyotes, jackals, dingoes, wild dogs, and domestic dogs) can interbreed. Foxes can also breed with other canids, but they rarely do. The DNA makeup of all canids is almost identical, which is one reason why all canids share characteristics like a sixty-three-day gestational period and forty-two teeth.

So, maybe we should start viewing cats and dogs as relatives, not rivals. Then again, don't relatives compete and quarrel sometimes?

Did You Know?

The board game known as Hounds and Jackals was a favorite of the ancient Egyptians. The game first appears in records from 1300 BCE. A board for the game, along with ten game pieces, was found in an ancient tomb from that era.

"Long life to you!
Good health to you and your household!
And good health to all that is yours!"

I SAMUEL 25:6

22

WHY YOU LOOK LIKE YOUR DOG

Have you ever been told you look like your dog? (For many of us, this is a compliment!) If so, there is some science to back up the similarity. Humans and dogs share about 90 percent of their genetic codes. This might explain the close bond between dogs and people.

However, the genetic similarity also means that 60 percent of genetic disorders in dogs correspond to genetic diseases in humans. These conditions include blindness, cancer, epilepsy, congenital heart disorders, deafness, and neurological abnormalities.

Several years ago, the Broad Center/MIT Center for Genome Research released a detailed genome map of a female boxer named Tasha. Tasha's genome sequence was posted on the Internet, allowing researchers to use her data to research both canine and human genetics. This is just one more example of how humans and dogs have helped and learned from one another over the past several thousand years.

Speaking of Dogs . . .

"Dogs are the leaders of the planet. If you see two
life forms, one of them is making a poop, the other one's
carrying it for him, who would you assume is in charge?"
Jerry Seinfeld

A friend loves at all times.
PROVERBS 17:17 NKJV

23

THE QUEEN OF DOGS AND CATS

Queen Victoria is known for many things (including the tradition of brides wearing white for their weddings). Further, when U.S. President Abraham Lincoln was assassinated, the queen set the standard for reaching out to someone in grief. A widow herself, Her Majesty wrote a touching letter to Mary Todd Lincoln. She included these words: "I earnestly pray that you may be supported by Him to whom Alone the sorely stricken can look for comfort in this hour of heavy affliction." She signed the letter, "I remain, dear Madam, your sincere friend Victoria."*

It's no surprise that a woman with such a tender heart was an animal lover. Queen Victoria was instrumental in restoring the domestic cat to its former glory (after years of being maligned as a minion of the dark side). The queen loved her cats, and, through her example and her words, she helped rebuild the domestic cat's sterling reputation as a playful, loving, and clever companion.

In an effort to help dogs and cats (and other animals too), in 1840 the queen renamed the Society for the Prevention of Cruelty to Animals, as the Royal Society for the Prevention of Cruelty to Animals—its current moniker. This decision marked more than a name change. Before Queen Victoria's endorsement, many people scoffed at animal welfare, as they didn't consider dogs and cats to be sentient beings. Because of her involvement,

---

* More of the letter from Queen Victoria to Mary Todd Lincoln can be found in the excellent biography *A. Lincoln: A Biography*, by Ronald C. White Jr. (New York: Random House, 2009).

organized animal welfare became seen as an important and legitimate effort. (What happened in Britain also set the stage for the American Society for the Prevention of Cruelty to Animals [ASPCA], which was founded by Henry Bergh in 1868.)

During the early part of her reign, the queen's favorite pet was a Cavalier King Charles spaniel named Dash. She wrote a heartfelt epitaph for Dash when he passed away, stating that even though the affectionate and playful little spaniel was no longer physically present, he "still lives beloved."

Did You Know?

Cavalier King Charles spaniels have a long history of popularity with British monarchs. In addition to Queen Victoria, at least three Stuart kings owned this breed. Because they were immersed in stiff formality and etiquette, many rulers found delight in an unassuming and unabashedly affectionate dog, whose eyes seem to say, "Hi, I love you! Let's play!"

👓

For the LORD comforts his people
and will have compassion on his afflicted ones.

ISAIAH 49:13

DOGS: MESSENGERS OF GOD?

You might know that cats were revered in ancient Egypt. Dogs were equally esteemed. Canine companions began to appear in Egyptian artwork in 4500 BCE. From art and literature, we know that dogs were well respected in Egypt—and considered by some to be special heavenly messengers.

Egyptians kept dogs, like Salukis, as companions and hunting partners. They also used mastiffs in battle. It was not uncommon for dogs to be mummified and buried with honor. When a family's dog died, the owners shaved their heads—indeed, their whole bodies—as a sign of mourning.

Many Egyptians wanted to be buried with their dogs because they believed that humans and their beloved canines should share both life and afterlife together. The Egyptians understood the timeless truth that one lifetime is not enough to spend with a cherished canine friend.

Speaking of Dogs . . .

"God created angel dogs to help us live better and happier lives."
John Paul DeJoria

👓

Light in a messenger's eyes brings joy to the heart.
PROVERBS 15:30

25

THE GEESE POLICE

Is your dog an enthusiastic bird-chaser? So much so that she could make a career of it? If you have a gun dog or a herding dog, there might be a job waiting for her—in the Geese Police! These dogs are taught to chase birds from airport tarmacs in an effort to keep "bird strikes" to a minimum.

Bird strikes occur when a flock of birds collides with an aircraft. The birds can be sucked into a plane's engine, causing mechanical failure or damaging the craft's wings. According to the Federal Aviation Administration, bird strikes are a serious safety issue, occurring at a rate of about two thousand per year with commercial airliners.

Border collies and other breeds are also used to banish geese, gulls, and other birds from parks, golf courses, ball fields, hotels, and auto dealerships—anywhere that bird excrement or aggressive behavior can be a health/safety hazard or a simple nuisance.

Did You Know?

A brave, Russian bear-hunting breed is used to protect humans from bear encounters in public. Karelians intimidate bears, warning them that interacting with humans and invading their environment is not a good idea. Even though Karelians were bred to hunt bears, they are actually helping bears; if a bear regularly invades human-occupied areas, it often ends up being euthanized.

Love … always protects.

1 CORINTHIANS 13: 1, 7

26

WORK LIKE A DOG?

It's a special day that gives new meaning to the phrase "working like a dog." It's Take Your Dog to Work Day (TYDTWD), which is celebrated on the Friday following Father's Day. (Take Your Dog to Work Day 2017 will be on June 23.)

The event encourages employers to experience the joy that pets bring to the workplace. Created by Pet Sitters International in 1999, TYDTWD also promotes dog adoption, as people witness firsthand the special bond between dog lovers and their pets. And it encourages employers to offer pet-friendly benefits to employees.

For more information, including an event tool kit and tips for integrating your dog into workplace/office life, visit TakeYour Dog.com.

Incidentally, a survey conducted by dogfriendly.com revealed that 14 percent of respondents take their dogs to work *every* day.

Did You Know?

According to the Humane Society of the United States (HSUS), one in five family dogs was adopted from an animal shelter. (By the way, 25 percent of dogs in animal shelters are purebreds.)

All hard work brings a profit.

PROVERBS 14:23

27

DOG STARS

From Rin Tin Tin back in the 1920s to Benji in the 1970s and Uggie in more modern times, dogs have been a staple on the big and small screens. Many dogs used in television and film are rescued from animal shelters or similar organizations, with animal trainers rescuing dogs and launching them into lifelong careers. Eddie, the Jack Russell terrier who first gained fame on TV's *Frasier*, is a great example. Even after *Frasier*, Eddie worked nearly nonstop.

The American Humane Association (AHA) oversees the treatment of dogs and other animals in TV and film. The AHA, which formed in 1940, has a contract with the Screen Actors Guild to monitor the treatment of animal actors on set, working closely with producers and animal trainers to review safety measures and living conditions during production time. Programs and movies that are deemed acceptable by the AHA qualify for an official end-credit notation. (Look for this when the credits roll next time you watch a movie or TV show.) Then, when a dog star retires, he or she is re-homed with an adoptive family. (Ethical dog trainers never return a dog to an animal shelter.)

To see AHA ratings of current movies, visit AHAfilm.org.

Speaking of Dogs . . .

"I want to love like a dog, with unabashed devotion
and complete lack of concern about what people do
for a living, how much money they have, or how much
they weigh. The fact that we still live with dogs,
even when we don't have to herd or hunt our dinner,
gives me hope for humans and canines alike."

Oprah Winfrey

👓

Those who are wise will shine like the brightness
of the heavens, and those who lead many
to righteousness, like the stars for ever and ever.

DANIEL 12:3

28

SMELLS LIKE A JOB FOR A DOG

Have you ever marveled at your dog's sense of smell? How did
he find that old piece of pizza crust he hid in the back of the
closet—seven months ago?

Dogs have olfactory skills that beat humans by way more
than a nose. That's why detection dogs work for the armed
forces, police departments, health organizations, and more. Dogs

can be trained to sniff out contraband drugs, weapons, explosives, currency, and banned agricultural products.

And termite-tracking dogs are hired by pest-control companies. Beagles are expert termite-busters. They can find termites under floors, in soil, and within walls. In one test at the University of Florida, a group of dogs was found to be 95 percent accurate in locating termites.

Dogs can also find mold in the walls of a house or other building, detect melanoma cells on human skin, and help find missing people. And new research indicates that a dog might be able to detect lung cancer in humans, just by smelling their breath.

Did You Know?

How keen is a dog's sense of smell? Your dog can smell the ketchup on your hamburger, and we mean every *individual* ingredient in that ketchup. A dog can zero in on the vinegar amid the competing smells of tomato paste, onion powder, and corn syrup.

6ô

"Remember, Lord, how I have walked
before you faithfully and with wholehearted devotion
and have done what is good in your eyes."

ISAIAH 38:3

29

ONE FAST ROTTIE

Becky Buffum of Austin, Texas, knows that appearances can be deceiving. Her Rottweiler, Cassidy, is missing one leg, but that hasn't slowed her down a bit. She excels on agility and lure courses, and she won a fastest dog contest, sprinting at nineteen miles per hour. That's as fast as an elite high school sprinter. Unless you are a very good runner, you would struggle to keep up with Cassidy in a race across your local football field.

Becky and Cassidy regularly visit retirement homes and schools, where Cassidy serves as a therapy dog, reminding the young and the old that one fast look doesn't allow us to truly *see*.

Did You Know?

Therapy dogs like Cassidy the Rottweiler are used to console and comfort people dealing with disaster, trauma, or other life challenges. Therapy dogs have calmed children after a school shooting, provided friendship and comfort to firefighters while they combat forest fires, and helped in the recovery of victims of earthquakes, tornadoes, and hurricanes.

Calmness can lay great offenses to rest.

ECCLESIASTES 10:4

Top 10 Least Popular Biblical Names for a Dog

10. Ananias
9. Sapphira
8. Pontius
7. Kevin
6. Methuselah
5. Jehoshaphat
4. Jezebel
3. Bathsheba
2. Mephibosheth
1. Judas

(Honorable Mention: Whore of Babylon, Herod, James the Lesser, Bildad the Shuhite, and Tricia.)

30

WARTIME SACRIFICE

Would you let your dog "volunteer" for military service? Dogs have been used in war throughout history. The ancient Romans and Greeks used mastiffs in battle, outfitting them with spiked collars to make them look even fiercer.

During the American Revolution, soldiers routinely brought their hunting dogs with them into battle, where they served as watchdogs as well as companions/comforters. Many years later, during World War II, American dogs were actively solicited for military duty. Most of the dogs who served were loaned by patriotic families who wanted to help in the effort. About nineteen thousand dogs were recruited, and 55 percent of them passed their training and proceeded into service. They served as patrol dogs, scout dogs, and guard dogs.

After the war, most of the surviving dogs were returned to their families. These canine volunteers saved thousands of lives during the war. In Guam, twenty-five Marine Dobermans died in the line of duty. A life-sized sculpture of a Doberman now memorializes their service.

Did You Know?

U.S. military dogs serving in Afghanistan and Iraq have special needs due to the dry climate and blowing sand. Many of the dogs have suffered from corneal ulcerations and conjunctivitis. Fortunately, a donation of Doggles, protective eyewear for dogs, has made a huge difference. Army vets and dog handlers say the measure has dramatically reduced the amount of canine eye trouble.

👓

My eyes stay open through the watches of the night,
that I may meditate on your promises.

PSALM 119:148

31

AN ABLE GUIDE

Today, we see guide dogs everywhere, but they were virtually unknown in the United States until a landmark *Saturday Evening Post* article in 1927. Two years later, the first U.S. guide dog organization, The Seeing Eye, launched.

The popularity of guide dogs spiked after World War II, when soldiers who were blinded in battle wanted to find a way to retain or regain their independence. The original guide dogs were German shepherds, who are strong, agile, intelligent, and highly trainable (the same traits that make them fine police dogs). Today, guide dogs are often Labrador or Golden retrievers, poodles, or boxers.

Contrary to common perception, guide dogs do not lead their handler. Instead, the handler tells the dog where to go, and the dog looks out for obstacles. These canines are trained to "intelligently disobey." For example, the handler might tell the dog to cross the street, but the dog will note a car speeding around a corner and stop the handler from proceeding. The dog will even step into the handler's path if necessary.

By the way, if you ask if you can pet a guide dog and the handler turns you down, don't be offended. Distracting a guide dog can be dangerous or confusing for the dog and his handler. When a dog dons his harness, things are all business. Even when lying under a restaurant table, a guide dog (or therapy dog) has been trained to avoid licking or scratching himself. He can't even eat fallen crumbs.

Did You Know?

Many guide dogs are bred, raised, and trained by nonprofit organizations. It takes several months to train a guide dog, and after this training, a dog is carefully matched with a handler. Once this match is made, a dog and his handler are partners for the rest of the dog's working life.

Two are better than one,
because they have a good return for their labor.

ECCLESIASTES 4:9

32

STORMY TIMES FOR DOGS

When the thunder rolls and lightning cracks, does your dog whine, pace, or hide under the dining room table? Some breeds, such as herders like collies and German shepherds, seem predisposed to fear storms. Ditto for hounds, like beagles and bassets, and sporting dogs, like pointers, setters, and spaniels.

Animal behaviorists are unsure what frightens dogs most when it storms. Is it the booming thunder, the bright lightning, the howling wind, or the drumming of rain or hail on the roof? It's possible that these dogs might be reacting to a change in air pressure or electrical charges in the air. After all, some dogs become upset well before a storm actually hits.

If your dog is storm sensitive, consult a veterinarian or animal trainer. He or she might suggest a therapy such as DAP, or dog-appeasing pheromone. Pheromones are biological or chemical substances that influence behaviors in animals. DAP is a specific pheromone that mimics the pheromones produced when a female dog lactates. Used in conjunction with behavior modification measures, DAP can help ease a dog's anxieties. DAP is available as a spray or a diffuser that can be plugged into an electrical outlet.

Did You Know?

Feeling like you are your dog's personal doorman or doorwoman? Don't let him dictate when he enters your home. Ignore the scratching, barking, and whining. Open the door only when the dog is calm (even if the weather outside is not so calm).

∙ ∙

6∂

He stilled the storm to a whisper.

PSALM 107:29

33

THE FREE DOGS OF CONSTANTINOPLE

L ong ago in Constantinople (modern-day Istanbul, Turkey), stray dogs were so plentiful that the Turks regarded them as a class of citizen. According to popular legend, these Free Dogs were allowed have the run of Constantinople, to honor them for helping defend the city from a night-time invasion. In addition to all the freedom, the Turks gave the dogs shelter and food, feeding them offal and porridge scraps.

Over time, the Free Dogs began to resemble their human benefactors. They formed armies, each with a clear leader. These armies often battled one another for supremacy. By some estimates, the number of Free Dogs reached thirty thousand. But the large number didn't mean the dogs were anonymous. Some villagers left bequests to make sure the Free Dogs on their streets were cared for after their death.

During the early days of the American continent, dogs were bred and trained to work in a variety of jobs. Dogs herded and guarded livestock, pulled carts laden with people and goods, and operated grain wheels. They also served as hunters, rescuers, and even soldiers in war.

6∂

Be agreeable, be sympathetic, be loving,
be compassionate, be humble.

I PETER 3:8 MSG

34

A BREED APART?

Many dog lovers are loyal to a particular breed. However, these folks are sometimes surprised to learn that different dog breeds are not different species.

All domestic dogs are members of the species *Canis familiaris*. Even breeds that look very different are, essentially, the same. The Rhodesian ridgeback and the Chihuahua are cut from the same cloth, genetically speaking. In fact, if dogs of ten different breeds were invited to breed for several generations, the resulting dogs would look basically the same as their great-great-great grandparents.

Scientists have learned that the limited genetic diversity in a given breed can make purebred dogs susceptible to genetic diseases. When breeders develop a dog breed and enter that breed into a registry, the "stud book" is closed, meaning that only specific dogs can mate to create descendants of the breed. So, if a particular breed becomes very popular or is affected by disease or some other factor, the breed's existence is threatened.

For example, the Lundehund (or puffin hound) was almost wiped out during World War II, due to an outbreak of distemper on the small island where the breed was developed. By the war's end, fewer than twelve Lundehunds remained. The breed survived, but its small gene pool has led to a genetic intestinal disorder so common that it's called Lundehund syndrome. It affects more than 70 percent of puffin hounds. Fortunately, DNA-mapping research has led to better breeding, as mutated genes can be eliminated from future breeding efforts.

Did You Know?

The first dog genome sequence was unveiled in 2003 by scientists at the Institute for Genomic Research and the Center for Advanced Genomics. This landmark genome belonged to a family pet, a standard poodle named Shadow.

😎

God blessed them and said, "Be fruitful and multiply.
Fill the earth and govern it. Reign over the fish
in the sea, the birds in the sky, and all the animals
that scurry along the ground."

GENESIS 1:28 NLT

35

UNCOMMON DOGS

The dog as a status symbol is nothing new. In medieval Europe, dogs served as hunters and were cherished by the nobility of the day. A well-heeled European might own hundreds of dogs. In fact, these hunting hounds were so valued that the common people were not allowed to have dogs who could course or pursue game. If you were a commoner, your dog would have to be under a certain size—or be hobbled so that you and your canine could not poach a deer or rabbit from the land-owning gentry.

Enter the terrier group. According to some historians, the common folk began breeding dogs that were small enough to be legal but keen and skilled enough to hunt small prey. Ironically, by the time the Renaissance rolled around, dogs were still a status symbol among European royalty, but not all of them were hunting dogs. The royals, possibly inspired by the hoi polloi, began to breed small dogs as companions. These dogs didn't hunt; they were pampered members of the aristocracy, and they lived in the lap of luxury, literally and figuratively.

Did You Know?

Some of the small dogs of the Renaissance were gallant warriors. Despite their diminutive stature, they didn't hesitate to fight much larger opponents. (The canine spirit of bravery is reflected in recent cases in which a Doberman and a golden retriever both fought off mountain lions in defense of home and family.)

"The LORD does not look at the things people look at.
People look at the outward appearance,
but the Lord looks at the heart."

1 SAMUEL 16:7

YOU CAN'T CATCH COOTIES FROM YOUR DOG

Cooties, that mysterious condition that has hampered many a schoolyard romance, is real. Cooties are lice—parasitic insects that like to dwell on humans and many other warm-blooded creatures, including your pet dog or cat.

Body lice (what are commonly called cooties) are truly something to be feared by children and adults alike, as they can spread typhus fever. However, you don't need to fear procuring lice from your dog, and vice versa. Lice are species specific. Lice called *Trichodectes canis* and *Linognathus setosus* infest dogs, while *Felicola subrostrata* is the only kind that infests cats. None of these also infect humans.

Incidentally, the term cootie might spring from the Malay word *kutu*, which means "biting insect."

Speaking of Dogs . . .
"Dogs never bite me. Just humans."
Marilyn Monroe

🕶

And so the word of the Lord [regarding salvation]
was being spread through the entire region.

ACTS 13:49 AMP

37

DOGS WITH SOUL

Do dogs have souls? This question isn't even debatable for many dog lovers. However, theologians have wrestled with some version of "Do dogs go to heaven?" for thousands of years.

In early Judaism, for example, dogs were considered unclean. But other ancient peoples, like the Egyptians, believed dogs have souls. They manifested this belief by burying dogs with their owners—for protection and companionship in the afterlife. Some Egyptians took things even further, worshiping canine demi-gods.

Eventually, Judaism warmed to the idea that God and dog could co-exist spiritually. According to Judaic lore, dogs earned spiritual kudos for remaining silent when the Israelites began their exodus from Egypt. Further, the Talmud praises dogs for their faithfulness to and protection of their masters. For example, it is written that God gave Adam's son Cain a dog as a symbol of divine mercy and protection.

Did You Know?

Dogs are often portrayed in nativity scenes, along with various barnyard animals. Some Christians believe that dogs accompanied the New Testament wise men and the shepherds on their journeys to visit the Christ Child. (All told, dogs are mentioned twenty-four times in the Bible.)

6ð

You are my hiding place;
you will protect me from trouble
and surround me with songs of deliverance.

PSALM 32:7

38

GOING GREEN WITH YOUR DOG

Most pet owners are cautious with household cleaners and candles, but many common houseplants and produce are also toxic or irritating to dogs. From avocados and eggplant to hyacinth and tiger lilies, the list of toxic plants is longer than most people think.

"Many plants, both in the house and the yard, can be toxic to our pets," says Dr. Tina Wismer, DVM. "Some toxic plants cause only mild stomach upset, but others can be poisonous. As a pet owner, it's important that you be familiar with the most dangerous of the toxic plants—like Sago Palms, Easter lilies, Japanese yews, and azaleas."*

For a complete list, visit the Humane Society's website (hsus. org) or ask for a list from your veterinarian. This will help you know which flora to avoid or to place in a dog-free zone in your home.

Did You Know?

Some veterinarians now recommend canine products featuring CBD (cannabidiol), which is one of two main ingredients found in cannabis. CBD, which is extracted from hemp rather than from marijuana plants, is different from THC, the substance that makes users high. CBD is said to be an anti-inflammatory and a pain reliever, and some studies have shown CBD to be effective for other ailments, like epileptic seizures. CBD is found in products like Therabis, which was developed by New York veterinarian Dr. Steven Katz. Of course, you should always consult your veterinarian before giving a dog any new medication.

ᏬᏅ

He makes grass grow for the cattle,
and plants for people to cultivate—
bringing forth food from the earth.

PSALM 104:14

---

* Visit vetstreet.com for more information on Dr. Wismer.

Dog-Safe Greenery

Here is one list of dog-safe plants. For a more complete list, ask your vet or visit a trusted website, such as the Humane Society (hsus.org) or the ASPCA (aspca.org).

Alfalfa sprouts
Areca palm
Begonia
Catmint
Chamomile
Dahlia
Lemon button fern
Oregano
Ponytail palm
Sage
Spider plant
Thyme
Zinnia

39

DOG INNS ARE IN!

The traditional hotel-chain industry is facing challenges, but specialized pet hotels are booming. The dog spa chain Dogtopia now boasts more than twenty-five locations, and the luxury D Pet Hotels has opened in trendy Hollywood, Scottsdale, and Manhattan. Pets R Inn has locations in five states.

So, what makes a pet hotel different from a mere pet-friendly hotel? Well, the latter is for humans with pets in tow while the former offers upscale accommodations for pets only.

For example, at Auntie Barbara's Bed, Bath & Biscuit in Lowell, Indiana, canine guests enjoy temperature-controlled rooms, beds and pillows (as long as they are not used as chew toys), and a house call from a veterinarian who specializes in doggie acupuncture and chiropractic. Meanwhile, the national Pooch Hotel chain features swimming pools—with lifeguards. Pooch Hotels also offer a doggy spa, complete with aromatherapy, a "paw-dicure," and a Poochberry facial.

For felines, the Holiday Pet Barn resorts in Virginia offer cats "furrmazing" multi-level condos with special features such as a private hidden potty, a built-in aquarium with moving fish, and a state-of-the-art ventilation system. At these resorts, cats also receive a "compawssion hug" twice a day.

It seems we humans may economize on many leisure expenses, but not on the comfort of our four-footed friends.

Speaking of Dogs . . .

"Heaven goes by favor. If it went by merit,
you would stay out and your dog would go in."

Mark Twain

👓

The fear of the LORD leads to life;
then one rests content, untouched by trouble.

PROVERBS 19:23

40

PAUSE FOR PAW CARE

I f you can hear your dog's toenails clicking on your floor or the
sidewalk, it might be time for a pet pedicure. Smart dog lovers
know that dogs should be walking on their paw pads, not their
toenails. When a dog's nails grow too long, it increases the possibility of a nail breaking or catching on something, like a loop of
loose carpet, and getting pulled off.

A dog's nails should be clipped or filed every one to three
weeks. In addition to the safety benefits already named, keeping
those nails short will prevent premature canine arthritis. Similar
care should be taken with a dog's pad hair. No matter the age, a

dog needs the hair between the foot pads to be kept short. Doing so will keep your canine from bringing outside messes inside (you know what we mean). More important, well-trimmed hair will keep a dog from falling and getting hurt, especially when dashing across slippery floors and other surfaces.

Seen in a Church Bulletin

Next week's "Bring Your Dog to Church Day" has been canceled, due to an outbreak of common sense.

👓

Do you not know that in a race all the runners run,
but only one gets the prize?
Run in such a way as to get the prize.

I CORINTHIANS 9:24

41

LIONS AND FO DOGS

According to Buddhist legend, Buddha owned a lion, which he trained to obey him like a faithful dog. This "Fo Dog" became a symbol of the religion, and we often see the leonine Fo Dogs (also called Foo Dogs) at the entrances of Buddhist temples and some Asian restaurants. This is one reason why lions are so well respected in India, Buddha's birthplace.

However, when Buddhism spread to China, where there are virtually no lions, a new symbol was needed. Enter a dog that looked like a lion: the Pekingese. The Han emperor Ming Ti noted that the Pekingese closely resembled a lion (at least to his eyes), so he dubbed the breed the Lion Dog (or Fo Dog).

Eventually, in countries like Tibet and Japan, breeds like Lhasa Apsos, Tibetan spaniels, and shih tzus were also called Fo Dogs. These breeds were considered royalty, and, in China, could live only within the walls of the Forbidden City. One emperor, Ming of the Tang Dynasty, loved his Pekingese so much that the two were legally married.

Did You Know?

In Chinese astrology, the Year of the Dog occurs every twelve years. The next Year of the Dog will be 2018. According to lore, people born during this year are loyal, honest, affluent, critical, and sometimes aloof. Year of the Dog people are believed to be strong leaders.

The righteous are bold as a lion.

PROVERBS 28:1 NKJV

42

A PULITZER WINNER AND HIS DOG

"A sad soul can kill you quicker, far quicker, than a germ."
—John Steinbeck

John Steinbeck, the college drop-out turned Pulitzer Prize-winning novelist, is revered for fiction works like *The Grapes of Wrath*, *Cannery Row*, and *Of Mice and Men*. But for many dog lovers, Steinbeck's nonfiction masterwork, *Travels with Charley*, stands above all the rest.

Charley was Steinbeck's standard poodle who joined the author for a 1960 cross-country road trip, from Long Island to the Pacific Coast. According to Steinbeck's children, the author knew his health was failing and wanted to see his country one last time. And what better companion than his beloved dog?

Charley's exploits pepper the book. For example, Steinbeck writes, "Once Charley fell in love with a dachshund, a romance racially unsuitable, physically ridiculous, and mechanically impossible. But all these problems Charley ignored. He loved deeply and tried dogfully."

Speaking of a Dog Named Charley . . .

"Sir, this is a unique dog. He does not live by tooth or fang. He respects the right of cats to be cats, although he doesn't admire them. He turns his steps rather than disturb an earnest caterpillar. His greatest fear is that someone will point out a rabbit and suggest that he chase it. This is a dog of peace and tranquility."

John Steinbeck

· ·

68

Fix these words of mine in your hearts and minds. ...
Teach them to your children, talking about them when
you sit at home and when you walk along the road. ... Write
them on the doorframes of your houses and on your gates.

DEUTERONOMY 11:18–20

43

MISCONCEPTIONS ARE THE PITS

Are you breaking the law just by owning a dog or two? (Or three?) You might be, especially if you have a Doberman, Rottweiler, mastiff, German shepherd, or pit bull in the family.

The so-called "breed bans" are laws (by county, city, neighborhood, state, etc.) that have arisen in response to the perceived threat presented by certain breeds of dog. Sometimes these laws are countrywide, such as Germany's banning of all "bully" breeds, like miniature bull terriers and American Staffordshire terriers.

Indeed, pit bulls are the targets of many breed bans at various government levels. (This is somewhat ironic, as some authorities, such as *The Original Dog Bible*, state that there is no such breed as the pit bull. Rather, the term refers to a group of canines who descended from the bull and terrier groups.) Among the dogs branded as pit bulls are the Staffordshire bull terrier, the

American Staffordshire terrier, the bull terrier, the American bulldog, and the Dogo Argentino. Because these dogs look somewhat similar, they are often lumped into the catch-all category of pit bull.

According to WebMD, there is only one technically true pit bull: the American pit bull terrier. However one might define the breed, the people who own pit bulls vociferously defend them. They point out that a well-bred and well-loved American pit bull terrier, for example, is as friendly as a Labrador retriever.

The ASPCA agrees. The organization's website notes, "A well-socialized and well-trained pit bull is one of the most delightful, intelligent, and gentle dogs imaginable."

Speaking of Dogs . . .

"All dogs can become aggressive, but the difference between an aggressive Chihuahua and an aggressive pit bull is that the pit bull can do more damage. That's why it's important to make sure you are a hundred percent ready for the responsibility if you own a 'power breed' like a pit bull, German shepherd, or Rottweiler."

Cesar Millan

ॐ

For sin shall no longer be your master,
because you are not under the law, but under grace.

ROMANS 6:14

WHERE THERE'S A WILL ...

You've probably read news stories of rich folks leaving piles of cash to their dog in their will. Makes sense, right? Most of us consider our dogs and cats to be family. So why can't a pet be the beneficiary of a will, just like children or grandchildren?

Consider the case of New York accountant Rose Ann Bolsany, who has bequeathed her million-dollar fortune to her Maltese terrier, Bella Mia (who eats filet mignon for dinner). Rose Ann calls Bella "a gift from God." Maybe that's why the five-year-old terrier is set to inherit a fortune that includes jewelry, a trust fund, and a vacation home.

But before you start to list Spot on that do-it-yourself will you found on the Internet, realize that, in the eyes of the law, your dog is property, not family. And one piece of property cannot own another piece of property, whether it's a bank account or a parcel of land.

Still, there is a way to care for your pet through wise estate planning. Loving pet owners can take steps to ensure that a canine or feline companion will be cared for in the event of death or incapacitation. In your will, you can name a guardian or set up a "pet trust" funded by proceeds of your estate. (Just make sure your chosen guardian is willing and able to take on the responsibility.)

Your attorney can advise you on the best way to ensure your pet's future comfort and well-being. Additionally, the HSUS provides information on how to write a will that protects pups. Visit their website, hsus.org, for more information.

"A dog doesn't care if you're rich or poor, smart or dumb.
Give him your heart, and he'll give you his."

Milo Gathema

6∂

Receiving a gift is like getting a rare gemstone;
any way you look at it, you see beauty refracted.

PROVERBS 17:8 MSG

45

SPAYING AND NEUTERING: FIXING THE MYTHS

Because pet owners are becoming more and more responsible, the number of homeless dogs and cats has dropped significantly over the past decade. However, pet overpopulation is still a huge problem in the United States. (Remember that a fertile dog can produce two litters in one year, and the average number of pups in a litter is six to ten.) According to the Humane Society, about six million dogs and cats enter shelters each year. About half of that number will end up being euthanized. (It's important to note that only 30 percent of dogs and 2 percent of cats in shelters are reclaimed by their owners.)

If all pet owners would spay or neuter their pets, the results could be truly amazing. We would be better able to care for the pets we have, and the number of dogs and cats competing for a good home would be reduced. If not "fixed," a dog and its mate (and the resulting offspring) could ultimately produce almost 66,000 dogs in six years.

Myths abound about the alleged down sides to getting a pet fixed. Here are a few of them, coupled with the truth:

1. **Dogs who are fixed get fat.** Most dogs are spayed or neutered when young, and, of course, they gain some weight as they grow and mature. Their metabolism slows just as a person's does. However, dogs who are fixed can maintain a healthy weight if they get regular exercise and are not overfed.

2. **In order to be well-adjusted, a female dog should have one litter before being spayed**. Uh, no. A female canine does not need to be a mom to be a happy dog. Further, having a litter contributes to the pet over-population problem and puts a dog at risk for certain types of cancer.

3. **Purebred dogs should reproduce**. As we mentioned before, one in four sheltered dogs is a purebred. Many of them came into the world under false assumptions like this one. Only responsible breeders with a well-planned program should be breeding purebreds.

4. **Spaying or neutering a dog damages its sexual identity**. Dogs are not people—at least not in the sexual-identity sense. A dog notices no difference in identity after being spayed or neutered.

Did You Know?

Dogs who have been spayed or neutered are less likely to roam about looking for love in all the wrong places. Further, these dogs are healthier because they are at less risk for developing cancer of the reproductive organs.

👓

Finally, brothers and sisters, whatever is true, whatever is noble, whatever is right, whatever is pure, whatever is lovely, whatever is admirable—if anything is excellent or praiseworthy—think about such things.

PHILIPPIANS 4:8

46

THE ART OF DOGS

From the cave drawings of North Africa to the computer-generated cartoons on modern sites like Tumblr, dogs have been featured in art for as long as there has been art.

Some of the first canine art depicts hunters and their skilled and loyal hunting dogs. The oldest of these works is a Persian drawing found in modern-day Iran. Dating to 7000 BCE, the work depicts a dog assisting its owner on a hunt. Later, in the Middle Ages, tapestries showing royal coursing dogs became popular.

In the 1800s, Sir Edwin Landseer often featured dogs,

especially black-and-white Newfoundlands, in his paintings. These superb water-rescue dogs are part of at least two of Landseer's works, "Off to the Rescue" and "Saved," which depict them in full rescue mode. In the latter painting, a Newfie rescues a child without any human assistance. Because of this connection between artist and subjects, black-and-white Newfoundlands are often called Landseer Newfoundlands.

Did You Know?

In the early 1900s, the cartoonist T. A. Dorgan drew a dachshund on a bread roll. The tube-shaped pup resembled a frankfurter, leading to the nickname "hot dog." However, the cartoon might also be an allusion to the rumor that frankfurters, which were a German addition to American menus, were made of dog meat.

And do not set your heart on what you will eat or drink.

LUKE 12:29

TOUGH SLEDDING FOR DOGS?

The annual Iditarod race, a thousand-mile-plus trek between Anchorage and Nome, Alaska, features sled dogs and their "mushers" braving frozen rivers, barren tundra, and steep climbs—amid temperatures that can plunge to fifty degrees below zero (Fahrenheit). A day when the mercury reads zero is considered mild.

Several breeds of dogs (or "athletes," as their owners call them) compete. The most common is the Alaskan Husky, a mixed-breed dog featuring Siberian Husky stock. The Alaskan Husky is bred for its stamina in the cold and for its deep love of running. Each sled is pulled by a highly trained team of twelve to sixteen canines. Two lead dogs head the pack, while the "wheel dogs" bring up the rear.

The Iditarod, while popular enough to be televised internationally, draws the ire of animal welfare groups like the Sled Dog Action Coalition. But dog-sled racing aficionados, especially mushers, counter that they take good care of their dogs. (Many of them even refer to their dogs as their children.) And they note that sled dogs *love* to run.

Musher and cancer survivor DeeDee Jonrowe points out that before competing in an Iditarod, she and her dogs have logged more than two thousand miles of training together. Jonrowe has won several awards during her career, including the Best Dog Care Award (presented by a team of veterinarians) and the Dog's Best Friend Award. She is a founding member of Mush with Pride, which aims to set standards for all aspects of sled-dog care—and for communicating with the public.

Organizations like Mush with Pride note that Iditarod dogs wear custom-designed booties to protect their feet from the terrain, and that each race includes checkpoints at which the dogs get a warm meal, vitamin supplements, and medical check-ups. Mushers add that many sled dogs live for twenty years or more because they are in such good shape. (According to PetMD, the average lifespan is eleven years for a small-breed dog and eight years for a large breed.)

It's true that the race is dangerous for the human and canine competitors; it's rare to have an Iditarod without a few bruises, abrasions, and broken bones. But perhaps the 2012 race is the best example of the bond between musher and sled dog. During the competition, Scott Janssen, a funeral home owner known as the Mushin' Mortician, saw one of his dogs, named Marshall, in dire straits. Janssen quickly performed mouth-to-snout resuscitation, saving Marshall's life.

What does all this mean for us "average" dog owners? We are not likely to have an Iditarod candidate in our household, but before entering our dogs in any competitions or beginning an exercise program (for example, bringing a dog along on a run), we should consult our veterinarians. Also consider your dog's age, breed, and overall health. When it comes to canine exercise, *exercise* common sense and knowledge.

Speaking of Dogs . . .

"Dogs are almost religion to me. They are the
best thing that ever happened to the human race.
Here is an animal that just loves. It doesn't give a darn
who you are or what you are. It doesn't care if you're rich,
if you're poor, if you're ugly. They just worship
you and will do anything for you."

Gary Paulson, Iditarod veteran

Do not run until your feet are bare and your throat is dry.

JEREMIAH 2:25

48

REALITY BITES

It's a fact: In the United States, almost five million people suffer a dog bite each year. And it is often children or other vulnerable people who incur those injuries. Even longtime dog lovers are surprised to learn that most bites happen to people the dog knows, even members of the immediate family.

Why do dogs bite? Reasons abound. Sometimes canines are afraid, sometimes they feel trapped, and sometimes they are ill or injured. Other dogs have a dominant temperament, which can be hereditary or something developed over time.

Here a few tips that dog lovers can use to put a muzzle on a biting problem:

1. If you buy a dog from a breeder, ask to meet the dam. Do not buy a dog if the mother is aggressive or overly fearful.
2. Spay or neuter your dog.
3. Do not allow your dog to nip or bite when playing.
4. When playing tug-of-war or other rambunctious games, maintain control of the activity. Teach your dog to drop the rope (or other object) on command.
5. Be cautious when bringing your dog into a new situation, such as meeting a new neighbor for the first time.
6. Discourage your dog from being possessive of food and toys. To help your dog understand that you are

the source of food, rather than competition for it, drop an occasional treat into its bowl during meal time.

7. Make sure your dog consistently follows your basic commands and responds when you call her name.

8. During puppyhood, or as early as possible, socialize your dog with many different sorts of people (for example, get your dog accustomed to small, inquisitive kids).

Did You Know?

Almost a third of liability claims against homeowners are related to dog bites or other aggressive animal behavior. As a result, some insurance companies will not provide coverage for large, powerful breeds such as Rotties, German shepherds, Dobermans, and pit bull types. If you own such a breed, double-check with your insurance company to clarify coverage.

Whoever eats sour grapes—
their own teeth will be set on edge.

JEREMIAH 31:30

49

FROM THE WOLF

Do you sometimes compare your dog to a wolf? If so, there's a good reason. According to some evolutionary biologists, the first semi-domesticated dogs date back to Ice Age Europe, about 32,000 years ago. These dogs evolved from the European wolf and would follow bands of semi-nomadic humans as they hunted woolly mammoths and other large prey. These early dogs scavenged the scraps left behind by their human benefactors.

Over time, a canine–human bond developed. The people provided food, and the dogs helped them locate prey and protected them from various carnivores. From this mutual respect, love evolved.

The European wolf became extinct thousands of years ago, but its descendants spread across the Old World and eventually to the Americas. Today's dog lovers should be grateful to the European wolf for the legacy of companionship and love that we enjoy today.

Did You Know?

Not all wolves are carnivorous pack animals. The South American maned wolf spends most of its life alone, and its diet consists mostly of fruit.

6∂

The wolf will live with the lamb, the leopard will
lie down with the goat, the calf and the lion and
the yearling together; and a little child will lead them.

ISAIAH 11:6

50

LIKE A DATING SITE FOR DOGS

The statistics on U.S. shelter dogs are sobering. Almost 2.3 million abandoned dogs are put to death every year; that's 6,276 dogs every day. As one might expect, younger and smaller dogs tend to be adopted more often than older and/or large dogs. At some overcrowded municipal shelters, a dog is often kept for only seventy-two hours, after which—if it is not claimed or adopted—the dog will be euthanized.

Enter Petfinder.com, a rescue site that looks a bit like a dating site. But instead of attractive singles (who might view one's picture and profile but never respond), this site features lovelorn canines who don't care what you look like or how much money you make. They just want to find a friend who will care about them and give them a good home.

Petfinder aggregates information about rescue animals available for adoption all over North America. The site features thousands of dogs looking for a "forever home," and has been a godsend for people like author Colin Campbell. After his wife left him, Campbell was encouraged by a friend to visit Petfinder. There, he found George, a 140-pound Newfoundland, whom he credits for "saving my life."

In his book *Free Days with George*, Campbell writes: "Within a year, we were inseparable—as George came out of his shell, his loving and gentle personality emerged and he made everyone he met smile, even me, and I had not smiled in over a year. I started to realize that he had rescued me even more than I had rescued him.

"When I was at my worst, George was there to comfort me. He taught me how to walk and how to wait, how to sit and be patient, and how to accept and embrace change. George gave me the knowledge and reassurance that even though you can be abandoned, you can still eventually find love and happiness again—dogs and people alike."

Did You Know?

The dog Nana, of *Peter Pan* fame, was a Newfoundland. Newfies are among the gentlest of all breeds and are revered for their nurturing nature with children.

👓

"Well done, good and faithful servant!
You have been faithful with a few things;
I will put you in charge of many things."

MATTHEW 25:23

51

PET FEARS

No one crafts conflict quite like legendary scare-meister author Stephen King, the man behind *The Shining*, *The Stand*, and *Cujo* (which featured one scary Saint Bernard on its cover).

"It might be," King once wrote, "that the biggest division in the world isn't between men and women but [between] folks who like cats and folks who like dogs."

King does not take sides in this age-old debate. His family has kept cats and dogs as pets. In one photo, one of King's cats sports a name tag that reads "Clovis." Clovis, as King fans know, is the name of the heroic cat in the author's screenplay for *Sleepwalkers*. A recent addition to the King family is Molly the Corgi, also known as The Thing of Evil. As King notes, "This wee little rump stumper is waddling straight into our hearts and she continues to try and fool us of her innocence with her contagious Corg smile."

For more information on Molly (and her author daddy), visit the Facebook page for Molly aka The Thing of Evil.

Did You Know?

According to Shawnee legend, a divine grandmother named Kohkumthena sits on a roadside, weaving a basket, which symbolizes her putting the finishing touches on the earth. But every night, this grandma's little dog unravels the basket. This mischief symbolizes the fact that the world is always in process.

6̄ə̄

The Lord is my light and my salvation—
whom shall I fear?

Psalm 27:1

52

DOG LOVE VERSUS CAT LOVE

It's a debate that seems as old as civilization itself: Who loves their humans more, cats or dogs? The answer: Both.

Here's the scoop: According to a study conducted at London's Lincoln University, your cat loves you and needs you—but not in the same way your dog does. "Although our cats were more vocal when their owners rather than a stranger left them [as part of the experiment]," note the study's authors, "we didn't see any additional evidence to suggest the bond between a cat and its owner is one of secure attachment."

The people behind the study are quick to point out that this does not mean that cats don't develop close relationships with their owners. They do. It simply means that the bonds cats form are not based on the dog-like need for security. This is likely because cats are independent hunters who are not as thoroughly domesticated as dogs.

While we humans eventually bred dogs to fit our needs, cats essentially moved in with us because the perks were good. Scientists have concluded that, even after almost nine thousand years of living with people, cats remain only "semi-domesticated." Moreover, dogs and cats have different social structures. Housecats "are not pack animals," notes Celia Haddon, author of *Cats Behaving Badly* and *How to Read Your Cat's Mind*, "so they are not going to depend on their owners. But it doesn't mean that they don't want to be around their owners. This study shows that they really do."

As for dogs, recent neuroimaging studies, such as one conducted at Atlanta's Emory University, reveal what many dog lovers have long suspected: dogs return the love they receive from their people. Moreover, dogs see us as family. They rely on humans even more than other dogs for affection, protection, companionship, and reassurance.

Speaking of Dogs (and Cats) . . .

"My idea of absolute happiness is to be in bed
on a rainy day, with my blankie, my cat, and my dog."

Anne Lamott

👓

"I truly understand that God shows no partiality,
but in every nation anyone who fears him and does
what is right is acceptable to him."

ACTS 10:34–35 NRSV

53

CALVIN THE DOG AND CAT LOVER

President Calvin Coolidge's affection for dogs and cats (and animals in general) was no political ploy designed to win the appeal of the pet-loving constituency. Coolidge was an animal fan from way back. As a young Vermont farm boy, he saved a litter of kittens from drowning. Cats and dogs had always been part of his life, so it was no surprise that our thirtieth president owned several cats in the White House. Their names were Smokie, Blackie, Tiger, Bounder, Timmie, and Climber (a Turkish Angora whom Coolidge nicknamed Mud).

As for dogs, the president was frequently photographed with his (reportedly) favorite pets of all, the white collies Rob Roy and Prudence Prim. Coolidge's presidential pet repertoire also featured birds, raccoons, a wombat, a bobcat, a pygmy hippo, and two lion cubs. The president and his wife, Grace, were so renowned as animal lovers that people began to send their unwanted pets to the White House.

Speaking of Dogs . . .

"Any man who does not like dogs and want them
about does not deserve to be in the White House."
President Calvin Coolidge

"How could your servant, a mere dog,
accomplish such a feat?"

2 KINGS 8:13

54

CHECKERS SAVES NIXON

It's one of life's great ironies: A canine can help humanize people. It's no wonder that public figures, especially politicians, make strategic use of a family dog to endear themselves to the public.

Consider the case of Richard Nixon and his cocker spaniel, Checkers. In 1952, Nixon was a U.S. Senator running for vice president along with presidential candidate Dwight D. Eisenhower. During the election season, Nixon was accused of accepting illegal political gifts and reimbursement funds, putting his position on the ticket in jeopardy. Nixon responded with a speech, which was seen or heard by more than sixty million people, a record at the time.

In the speech, Nixon denied wrongdoing and stated that the only gift he'd ever received from a lobbyist was Checkers—and that he would not return the spaniel, no matter what people said. He said that he and his children, who named the dog, loved Checkers too much to let him go.

This "Checkers Speech" brought forth an outpouring of public support, and the Eisenhower/Nixon duo won the election of 1952.

Did You Know?

President Lyndon B. Johnson's image was forever tainted in dog lovers' eyes when he tried to lift his beagle, Him, off the ground by the dog's ears. When Him yelped in apparent pain, so did much of the canine-loyal populous.

Like one who grabs a stray dog by the ears
is someone who rushes into a quarrel not their own.

PROVERBS 26:17

55

STUBBY THE WAR DOG

A bull terrier mix named Stubby served in World War I. But perhaps *served* isn't a good-enough word.

Stubby, a stray who was smuggled by troops onto a ship bound for France, is the most decorated war dog in U.S. history. He served for eighteen months in Europe, seeing action in seventeen battles on the Western Front. Once, he woke sleeping soldiers, using his keen sense of smell to warn of an incoming mustard gas attack. Thanks to Stubby, the soldiers had time to don their gas masks, which saved their lives. On another occasion, Stubby caught a German spy by the seat of his pants. Literally.

Because of his excellent hearing, Stubby regularly warned soldiers of incoming mortar shells. And his presence was a great comfort to wounded soldiers. During the war, the dog's heroic deeds regularly made newspaper headlines.

At the war's end, Stubby shook hands with President

Woodrow Wilson. He also met pet-loving presidents-to-be Calvin Coolidge and Warren G. Harding. General John Pershing presented Stubby with a gold medal made by the Humane Society, declaring the dog a "hero of the highest caliber."

He then toured the country and later became the mascot for Georgetown University. He died of old age in 1926 and is interred at the Smithsonian in Washington, D.C.

Speaking of Dogs . . .

"If a dog will not come to you after having looked you in the face, you should go home and examine your conscience."
President Woodrow Wilson

66

In all their distress he too was distressed, and the angel of his presence saved them. In his love and mercy he redeemed them; he lifted them up.

ISAIAH 63:9

56

WHO'S ALLERGIC TO WHOM?

While 10 percent to 30 percent of Americans are allergic to dogs and/or cats (depending on which allergist you believe), did you know that canines and felines can be allergic to people—sort of?

About 15 percent of all dogs suffer from allergies, and these canines can be allergic to dander, both from humans and felines. (Dander is the name for small cells shed from skin or hair.) This allergy usually doesn't make a dog sneeze or have watery eyes, but it can result in inflamed skin or itching.

And, according to one study, feline asthma, which affects one in two hundred cats, is on the rise. Human lifestyle is to blame. Because cats are more frequently kept indoors, they are more susceptible than dogs to inflammation of their airways caused by cigarette smoke, dust, human dandruff, pollen, and even some brands of cat litter.

So if your cat is wheezing and sneezing, or your dog is itchy and sore, you might be to blame. See your vet, if necessary.

Did You Know?

Chocolate contains a substance called theobromine, which is poisonous to cats and even more toxic to dogs.

I live and breathe God.

PSALM 34:2 MSG

OWNEY THE POST DOG

In the early 1890s, the U.S. Postal Service developed its own unofficial mascot.

During their rounds, postal workers in Albany, New York, noticed a homeless mixed-breed dog. They took him in, naming him Owney. Over the years of his unofficial postal worker career, Owney logged more than 140,000 miles with various mail carriers. He is most famous for his work with the Railway Mail Service, where he became a good-luck charm. In a day when train wrecks were common, no train with Owney as a passenger ever had a mishap.

Owney passed away in 1897, and his body was stuffed and put on display at the National Postal Museum in Washington, D.C., where it remains to this day as part of a display honoring him. He also has his own iPhone app, book, curriculum, and theme song (performed by country star Trace Adkins), and is "active" on Facebook and Twitter.

Did You Know?

The U.S. Postal Service is not the only agency to employ dogs. For example, the U.S. Department of Agriculture employs Jack Russell terriers in Guam. These terriers are trained to detect brown snakes and prevent them from being transported illegally in cargo shipments.

"If the home is deserving, let your peace rest on it."

MATTHEW 10:13

58

IT'S AN INVESTMENT, NOT AN EXPENSE

According to the market research company WSL, 81 percent of pet owners are spending the same amount of money, if not more, on their pets. "While they cut expenses in other areas of their household budgets, pet owners are still buying monogrammed sweaters, personalized food and water bowls, faux mink coats, and even Halloween costumes for their animals," notes WSL.

Indeed, pet supplies is a $63 billion industry that has been growing for the past twenty years according to AmericanPet-Products.org.

What are folks buying with those 63 billion bucks? Here are a few examples:

- Companies like Pet Saver make car seats that protect small dogs on road trips. Some of these seats face similar testing as those for child safety seats.

- Jogging strollers are not just for humans. Companies like Gen7Pets make pet strollers for canines up to seventy-five pounds. They can accommodate a variety of terrain.

- The Bike Tow Leash makes cycling with a dog fun and safe. This leash reduces the chances of tangling or tipping. It can also be used with wheelchairs. See biketowleash.com for more information.

- The tug toy known by the name MooTug gets its name from its source material. The toys are made from recycled rubber milking tubes from Minnesota dairy farms. (The faint scent of cow is a bonus for dogs—and their owners, if they grew up on a farm.)

Speaking of Dogs . . .

"Buy a pup and your money will buy love unflinching."
Rudyard Kipling

ᎶᎧ

You will increase my honor and
comfort me once more.

PSALM 71:21

59

HOW OLD IS YOUR DOG, REALLY?

One human year equals seven dog years, right? After all, that is the conventional wisdom. But savvy pet owners know that this would mean that a year-old dog, who is able to reproduce, is comparable to a seven-year-old child. And a fifteen-year-old dog, which is rather common, is like a 105-year-old person, which is uncommon, even with advances in medicine.

Here is a more realistic comparison: A three-month-old puppy is equivalent to a five-year-old child. A year-old dog is a human teenager of fifteen. A two-year-old dog is like a twenty-four-year-old person. After this milestone, the canine aging process slows, with each human year equaling four dog years. Thus, a four-year-old dog is thirty-six, and a ten-year-old dog is fifty-six. At fifteen, your dog is seventy-six. Some recalculation is necessary beyond his point, but, generally speaking, a dog who reaches twenty is like a ninety-three-year-old human.

So, that's the math. How you celebrate those doggy birthdays is up to you.

Did You Know?

With dogs, aging varies with breed. A Great Dane is considered an old-timer at seven, while a miniature poodle doesn't reach old age until eleven. Some breeds can still run agility courses at thirteen.

ᘎᘔ

"So the last will be first, and the first will be last."

MATTHEW 20:16

60

SIT ... STAY

Are you a pet lover with a travel bug?
If so, Rachel Martin and Andy Peck have a deal for you.

Back in 2010, Peck found himself pet sitting for three dogs and two cats—in a villa (complete with a vineyard and pool) in Spain. An idea was born. The idea? A service matching pet owners with sitters they could truly trust.

He and fiancée Rachel Martin spent the next two years testing and promoting the concept of exchanging a place to stay for animal care. You may have heard of their company, TrustedHousesitters, which is a network of more than fifty thousand members in one hundred and fifty countries. "There are millions upon millions of pet-owning households around the world for whom the worry of leaving a beloved animal at home or in boarding impacts how long, how often, and how they travel," notes Martin.

"It's a win-win," Peck adds. "Home-owners can travel with complete peace of mind that their home and pets are being cared for, while sitters can road-test different areas and save money on accommodation cost."

A pet-and-house-sitting gig can last from a few days to more than a year. The pets range widely as well. Beyond the dogs and cats are rabbits, horses, chickens, and alpacas. At press time, TrustedHousesitters has facilitated more than one million total pet-sitting nights.

Once sitters gain experience, they build up reviews from house-sitting clients and bolster their reputation and expand their opportunities for more gigs. "Not only is this a really brilliant way to travel, it's also a wonderful way to enjoy the company of pets," Martin says.

For more information, visit TrustedHousesitters.com.

Did You Know?

One of the sites listed on TrustedHousesitters.com is Markethill in the United Kingdom. This historic converted castle, which has been featured in the HBO series *Game of Thrones*, rests amid six hundred acres of forest. That's a lot of wandering territory for the castle's reigning monarchs, a dog and two cats.

Whoever seeks good finds favor.

PROVERBS 11:27

STAY CLASSY, LASSIE

There are enduring screen characters, and then there is Lassie. The world's most beloved collie starred on the big and small screens from 1943 to 2007, then enjoyed a renaissance in 2014 with the animated series *The New Adventures of Lassie*.

Many dog lovers know that Lassie was not a lass. The first to play the role was Pal, a "rough collie" protégé of expert dog trainer Rudd Weatherwax. Pal starred with Elizabeth Taylor and Roddy McDowell in 1943's *Lassie Come Home*, which was based on a 1938 *Saturday Evening Post* short story (which eventually became a novel).

Pal set the standard for future Lassies, who have all been male. Male collies retain a thicker coat in the summertime, when most filming is done. Further, the male dogs are larger by about ten to fifteen pounds. These factors make a dog look more imposing on screen. And it gave child actors, like Tommy Rettig and Jon Provost, longer careers, as they didn't tower over their co-star after just one season.

When Pal retired, he was replaced by Pal Junior, who eventually gave way to Baby, Pal's grandson, who filled the role for an impressive six years. All told, ten generations of Pal's direct descendants have portrayed Lassie in film and on television over more than sixty-four years.

There were seven Lassie movies before the TV version of the story debuted in 1954. TV's *Lassie* ran for nineteen years, making it one of the longest-running programs in television history.

Pal Junior's iteration of Lassie, representing the family legacy, received a star on the Hollywood Walk of Fame in 1960.

Did You Know?

While Lassie has always been played by a male dog, many of the Lassie stunt doubles were female. One additional note: Tommy Rettig, who played Jeff on the TV show, was allergic to dogs.

68

"And surely I am with you always,
to the very end of the age."

MATTHEW 28:20

62

PRESIDENTIAL DOGS AND CATS ...
AND RATS AND GATORS?

Y ou've read about some of the U.S. presidents who welcomed
dogs and cats to the White House (and you'll read about
more before we're done), but what's the total tally of Chief Exec-
utives who owned a canine or feline?

For cats, thirteen is the number—if you count Martin Van
Buren's tiger cubs. And we do.

Meanwhile, at least thirty-two of our presidents owned dogs
while on the job. Not surprisingly, Calvin Coolidge is the Dog
Lover in Chief. He had twelve dogs (and fourteen other assorted
critters) as pets during his presidency. His white collies were
the most photogenic, but rumor has it that his bulldog, Boston
Beans, was the most aromatic.

Incidentally, the White House has been something of a pet
menagerie through the years. Beside cats and dogs, presidential
pets have included pigs, goats, horses, snakes, rabbits, badgers,
cows, fish, geese, guinea pigs, hens, hamsters, roosters, sheep, lizards, a wallaby, a bear, a bobcat, a pygmy hippo, a ram, a flying
squirrel, a turkey, a donkey, a raccoon, and a piebald rat.

And let's not forget John Quincy Adams's pet alligator,
which he kept in the White House bathtub.

Among the forty-five presidents, Teddy Roosevelt is sec-
ond in the total-pet pack, with his total of twenty-three. John
F. Kennedy ranks a close third with twenty-one. In fact, only
Chester A. Arthur and Franklin Pierce failed to own some sort

of pet during their White House years. (Incidentally, the Teddy Roosevelt terrier, a type of vocal and athletic rat terrier, was named in honor of the twenty-sixth president, who owned several of them—one who reportedly ripped the pants off a visiting French ambassador.)

Another president, Millard Fillmore, didn't have an official pet at 1600 Pennsylvania Avenue, but he was rumored to regularly feed some stray cats, even inviting them into the East Room to sleep on a blanket during inclement weather. Furthermore, he was active in animal protection causes in his home state, New York. He started a branch of the Society for Prevention of Cruelty to Animals in Buffalo, the organization that would eventually become the ASPCA.

Fillmore explained his love for animals: "When I was a thoughtless boy, I took the life of a mother bird. I remember my father was greatly grieved and said, 'Millard, do you realize what you have done? You have taken the life of a mother, and have left her children to die of starvation in the nest. How would you like to have a great giant come along and kill your father and mother and leave you alone without food or care?' My father's rebuke sank so deeply into my heart that since that day I have never taken the life of a living creature."

Speaking of Dogs (and All Animals) . . .

"Becoming involved in animal protection means being prepared to meet the cold indifference of the thoughtless multitude, the ridicule and scoffs of the reckless, and the savage malignity of the cruel. But it is a good cause."

President Millard Fillmore

I led them with cords of human kindness,
with ties of love.

HOSEA 11:4

LEWIS AND CLARK ... AND SEAMAN THE NEWFOUNDLAND

Explorers Meriwether Lewis and William Clark had a special partner on their eight-thousand-mile adventure across the uncharted wilderness of the American West. When they began their trek in 1804, they brought along Seaman, a shaggy black Newfoundland. Seaman helped the duo by alerting them to grizzlies, hunting food, and (once) re-directing a buffalo who came charging into camp, saving several men from being crushed beneath its hooves.

Seaman suffered the hardships of the journey right along with his people. He nearly starved to death at one point (Newfies weigh up to two hundred pounds and have voracious appetites) and was bitten by a beaver.

Seaman is mentioned several times in Lewis and Clark's journals. However, no mention is made after July 6, 1806. No one is sure what became of Seaman, but it is evident that he was integral to the success of this historic exploration.

Did You Know?

Newfoundlands, like Lewis and Clark's Seaman, love the water. In Canada, the breed's country of origin, Newfies were used to tow lines and nets, and for water rescue. One Newfie pulled a lifeboat packed with twenty people to safety. Today, Newfoundlands are noted for their attempts to rescue swimmers, whether the swimmers need rescuing or not!

👓

The Lord will rescue me from every evil attack
and will bring me safely to his heavenly kingdom.

2 TIMOTHY 4:18

64

DO YOU KNOW DOG CPR?

Most responsible owners take their pets to a vet regularly. Some even have a dog and/or cat first aid kit. But what if your canine were having a breathing or heart problem? Is there such a thing as dog CPR?

Yes. And did you know that the American Red Cross conducts pet CPR classes? Dr. Deborah Mandell helped update the organization's course materials, and she hopes many pet owners will get up to speed on this life-saving procedure. Mandell works in the emergency room at the University of Pennsylvania's Matthew J. Ryan Veterinary Hospital, so she knows that pet CPR works. "I have definitely seen patients whose owners have performed CPR at home or in the car and have saved their pets," Mandell reports, "so I am a huge advocate, obviously, of having all pet owners know it."

Indeed, more than 60 percent of vet visits are emergencies, according to the American Animal Hospital Association. For more information on pet CPR, consult your veterinarian, the American Red Cross, or websites like aaha.org and vetstreet.com.

Also, the American Red Cross Pet First Aid app is available for both Android and iOS. It's a handy reference for many pet emergencies that you might encounter, and dog and cat lovers alike have downloaded it. Have you?

Did You Know?

The American Veterinary Medical Association now recommends acupuncture for many canine pain-related problems, including arthritis, joint disease, and epilepsy.

👓

Above all else, guard your heart,
for everything you do flows from it.

PROVERBS 4:23

65

WHAT KIND OF PERSON ARE YOU?

Are you a cat person or a dog person? Even if you answered, "Both," you probably have a preference. As it turns out, dog people and cat people truly do have different personalities, according to recent research.

In one study (conducted with six hundred college students and reported on the website Livescience.com), dog lovers tended to be more energetic and outgoing than cat lovers—and they were more likely to follow the rules rather than deviate from them. "It makes sense that a dog person is going to be more lively," says psychology professor Denise Guastello, one of the study's authors, "because he or she is going to be outside, talking to people, and bringing their dogs along. Whereas, if you're more introverted and sensitive, maybe you're more often at home, reading a book, because your cat doesn't need to go outside for a walk."

Cat lovers were 11 percent more likely to be introverts. They were also more open-minded and more sensitive than their canine-loving counterparts. Additionally, the research indicated that cat people tend to be non-conformists. Another finding is sure to heat up the rivalry among pet owners: Cat owners scored higher in intelligence than dog lovers.

However, no one connected with the survey could offer an explanation for this difference: Dog people usually cite Paul McCartney as their favorite Beatle, while cat lovers tend to prefer George Harrison.

๛

Make every effort to keep the unity of the Spirit
through the bond of peace.

EPHESIANS 4:3

66

RECESSION—PROOF PETS

According to the American Pet Products Association, pet ownership is one thing that is not trending downward in a tough economy.

More than 62 percent of Americans own pets, and we spend big on them, recession or no recession. We spent $43.2 billion in 2008, $47.7 billion in 2010, $53 billion in 2012, and $61 billion in 2013. When times are tough, having a dog or cat to cuddle goes a long way. That's one reason why almost seventy-nine million households have a pet—and almost half of all American households have more than one pet.

Pet services is a growing niche, with more than thirty-five chains providing everything from kitty and doggy daycare to grooming to dog walking. People are willing to cut corners, but not when it comes to pet care. Even picking up after pets has become big business. Witness the proliferation of chains like Pet Butler and Wholly Crap.

Pet ownership has been increasing by about 4 percent over the past several years, and the trend shows no sign of slowing down. According to multiple reports, the American population considers their pets to be part of the family. Indeed, almost 70 percent of parents confess that they treat their pets as well as they treat their children. This pet personification means that pet owners purchase holiday gifts, designer outfits, specialty shampoos, and high-tech gadgets like automated food dispensers.

As Jim Springston, a longtime dog owner, says, "It's not an expense; it's an investment in those we love."

Speaking of Dogs . . .

"My dogs aren't 'just like' members of the family.
They ARE members of the family."

Jim Springston

66

All honor to God, the God and Father of
our Lord Jesus Christ; for it is his boundless mercy
that has given us the privilege of being born again
so that we are now members of God's own family.

I PETER I:3 TLB

Top 10 Signs You Are a Dog Person

10. Your morning devotions consist of reading "Marmaduke" in the funny pages.

9. Your last Christmas letter included the term *ear mites*.

8. You win at Scrabble by busting out *Affenpinscher*.

7. Your family reunions are sponsored by Chuck Wagon.

6. You obsessively follow Boo the Pomeranian on Twitter.

5. Your Visa bill is dominated by purchases of organic rawhide bones and multi-colored dog wigs.

4. You've bid for a genuine Lassie hairball on eBay.

3. For your funeral, you've requested a dramatic reading from *The Hound of the Baskervilles*.

2. You recorded this year's International Dog Show—on your wedding DVD.

1. Your ring tone is just a long string of barks.

THE STORY OF LEX AND DUSTIN

In early 2007, U.S. Marine Corporal Dustin Lee, age twenty, found his base in Fallujah, Iraq, under mortar attack. A 73 mm rocket round exploded inside the base, injuring both Lee and his German shepherd bomb-sniffing companion, Lex. Despite suffering more than fifty shrapnel wounds, Lex refused to leave Lee's side. He had to be dragged away by medics so that the corporal could be flown to a hospital. Sadly, Lee, who had finished at the top of his military dog-handling class, died from his wounds.

After recovering from his own injuries, Lex continued to serve in the military. He worked as a therapy dog, visiting veterans at hospitals and retirement homes. After several months of service, Lex was allowed to retire so he could live out his days with Corporal Lee's family, at their earnest request. Late in 2007, eight-year-old Lex became the first working military dog to be granted an early retirement.

Lex received an honorary Purple Heart and the American Kennel Club Award for Canine Excellence. He lived at the Lee family home until 2012, when he died of cancer at age thirteen.

Speaking of Lex the Marine Dog . . .

"This is to certify that military working dog Lex, having served faithfully … is honorably discharged from the United States Marine Corps on this 21st day of December 2007."

An unnamed U.S. Marine at a ceremony for Lex

69

I said to myself, "Relax and rest.
God has showered you with blessings.
Soul, you've been rescued from death."
PSALM 116:7–8 MSG

68

OF DOGS, AND CATS ... AND BATS?

Fans of the classic comic book "Batman" know that Catwoman was a different breed of villain than the Caped Crusader's other foes, like the evil and murderous Joker, Riddler, and Penguin. Batman's creator, Bob Kane, crafted Catwoman as a foil who was not an evil killer. Instead, Catwoman was Batman's occasional love interest as well as his opponent. Kane described her as a "friendly foe who committed crimes but was also a romantic interest in Batman's rather sterile life." Catwoman engaged Batman in a high-stakes chess match as he tried valiantly to reform her.

For Kane, men like Batman resembled dogs, while women were more like the cats he knew. "Women are feline creatures," he explained, "while men were more like dogs. Dogs are faithful and friendly. Cats are cool, detached, and unreliable. Cats are as hard to understand as women are. We [men] don't want anyone taking over our souls, and women have a habit of doing that. So there's a love/resentment thing with women. With women, once the romance is over, somehow they never remain my friends."

Of course, dog devotees would tell Kane that a canine is always willing to try, and re-try, to make friends. Maybe that's why Batman never completely abandoned hope for Catwoman.

Did You Know?

According to renowned animal trainer Bash Dibra, "A dog responds to his owner's command because he is pack-oriented and considers his owner the leader. A cat doesn't respond to commands, because she doesn't understand them. A cat needs to be shown what is expected of her, or what is not acceptable, in more subtle ways."*

👓

In everything set them an example by doing what is good.

TITUS 2:7

A BIG, SMALL LOVE

Many dog owners have big love for their small Chihuahuas. However, "Chis" are a common breed at animal shelters, along with pit bulls and American Staffordshire terriers. In

---

* Bash Dibra, *Cat Speak* (New York: G. P. Putnam's Sons, 2001).

California and Arizona, shelters overflow with the pint-sized dogs, who, just like humans, are born with a soft spot on their heads.

Fortunately, people like actress Katherine Heigl are doing their best to bust myths about this breed. Heigl is proud mom to three rescued Chis (Gertie, Gracie Lou, and Poppie) and has teamed with the Helen Woodward Animal Center to launch a social media campaign dedicated to finding homes for Chihuahuas.

To join the campaign, visit animalcenter.org.

Speaking of Dogs . . .

"One loyal little dog is worth a big truckload of in-laws."
Taylor Morgan

68

For the Lord your God is a merciful God.
Deuteronomy 4:31

70

ALL IN THE FAMILY?

Did you get your dog from a friend or relative? According to the American Pet Product Manufacturers Association, almost 30 percent of single-dog households got their pet from a friend or relative. This number jumps to more than 52 percent in multiple-pet households.

Friends, family, and pets go together like peanut butter and jelly, marking a longtime American tradition. In 1785, George Washington received pet donkeys as a gift from King Charles III, the King of Spain. Abraham Lincoln's dog Fido often stayed in Springfield, Illinois, with family, while his president/owner was in Washington, D.C. More recently, the Obama family accepted a gift of a puppy, a Portuguese water dog named Bo, from their longtime family friend, the late Senator Edward Kennedy.

However, if you have a neighbor or uncle who *regularly* tries to gift you with a new puppy (or a donkey), the Humane Society recommends directing the person to a low-cost sterilization clinic (for the animal, not the human).

Did You Know?

In addition to cats and dogs, Abe Lincoln's White House was home to two pet goats, Nanny and Nanko. The president's sons Tad and Willie loved to tie carts or kitchen chairs to the goats and race them around the White House.

66

Share what you have with others.
God takes particular pleasure in acts of worship—
a different kind of "sacrifice"—that take place
in kitchen and workplace and on the streets.

HEBREWS 13:16 MSG

DOGS ARE FAMILY

Many of us dog lovers have fond memories of our childhood canines, and we'd like to pass on this shared experience to our children. However, pet ownership is more than a family tradition. Owning a dog (or two) can help a child learn love, respect, responsibility, and empathy.

By caring for a pet, a child gains a sense of accomplishment and personal competence. As responsible pet owners know, the way we care for our dogs, cats, etc., has real-life consequences. Kids can see the fruits of their labor in a happy, healthy dog. Further, they learn to value the idiosyncrasies, needs, and the very life of another creature who is sharing their living space.

Even a toddler can learn to handle the family dog gently, appreciating the dog's fragility but also its power. As a child grows older, he or she can be involved in feeding, grooming, administering medication or preventive treatments, or helping with a trip to the vet. In turn, kids find that they have a canine companion who will be loyal to them through thick and thin— or from algebra tests to broken hearts.

And of course, owning a dog helps us adults set a good example as we model patience and self-control and keep up with trends in nutrition, animal care, and veterinary medicine.

Learning about and caring for dogs can be a lifelong family labor of love. If done well, your children will carry on this sacred trust with their own families someday—with some very blessed dogs.

Speaking of Dogs . . .

"A dog changes coming home
to an empty house to coming *home*."
Drew Cody

6੭

I kneel before the Father, from whom every family
in heaven and on earth derives its name.

EPHESIANS 3:14–15

72

DOGS IN SPACE

During the famous "Space Race" between the United States
and the Soviet Union, the U.S.S.R. sent thirteen dogs into
space. The most famous of these was Laika, a stray dog who was
rescued off the Moscow streets and adopted by the Soviet space
program. She was launched into space on Sputnik II in 1957 and
was the first living animal to be sent into orbit. Sadly, she died
on her mission, and Americans and Soviets alike were outraged
when they learned that leaders of the Russian program had never
planned for Laika to return to earth alive.

The outrage was compounded decades later, in 2002, when
it was learned that the official story—that Laika died of oxygen

depletion during Sputnik's re-entry—was false. In fact, Laika died only a few hours into the mission when the cabin overheated.

Fortunately, most of the other early Soviet space dogs returned from space safely, due, at least in part, to Laika's sacrifice. In 2008, a monument to her was erected at the military facility where she was trained.

Did You Know?

The first cat in space fared better than Laika. The French feline Felicette, nicknamed Astrocat, rocketed into outer space in 1963. The cat was hooked up to sensors to monitor her vital signs and neurological activity. Thankfully, Felicette survived the trip.

𝟞𝟙

Be glad, good people! Fly to God!
Good-hearted people, make praise your habit.
PSALM 64:10 MSG

73

MANY HAPPY RETURNS

You have probably read of the struggles of U.S. service men and women who return from their tours of duty and struggle to adjust to life away from the battlefield. To dog lovers, it's no surprise that dogs are on the front lines of helping with this difficult transition.

The organization SARDUS (Search and Rescue Dogs of the United States) has teamed with the Returning Soldier Initiative to pair returning soldiers with dogs who meet national search-and-rescue standards. The program pairs a dog with a soldier and then provides training for both human and canine. Once a pair is good to go, they work with local law enforcement to look for lost or missing people.

For more information on PTSD or other reintegration challenges, visit returningsoldierinitiave.com or SARdogsus.org.

Speaking of Dogs . . .

"The friendship of a dog is precious. It becomes
even more so when one is so far removed from home. …
I have a Scottie. In him I find consolation and diversion.
He is the one person to whom I can talk without
the conversation coming back to war."
General Dwight D. Eisenhower

♋

"Be careful, keep calm and don't be afraid.
Do not lose heart."

ISAIAH 7:4

74

A MOST AMAZING BOND

It's a favorite story among dog lovers, one of the best examples of the amazing bond that grows between a dog and its human.

In the early 1900s, Hachiko, an Akita Ino, enjoyed life with his owner, Hidesaburo Veno, a professor at Tokyo University. Every workday, Veno would take the train from his home in Odete to Tokyo. And every day upon his return, he would find Hachiko waiting for him at Shibuya Station. The routine endured for years.

Then, in May of 1925, Veno passed away. This, no doubt, left Hachiko lonely and confused. But not without hope. For more than nine years, the Akita ventured to Shibuya Station every workday—at the same hour—hoping to greet Veno according to their custom. Hachiko faithfully made the journey until he too passed away.

This amazing story inspired the film *Hachi: A Dog's Tale* starring Richard Gere.

Did You Know?

"Some people would say dogs are loyal just because they depend on us for food and shelter, so they have to be nice to us. But when you see how dogs react when their humans and canine friends come back after they've been gone for a long time or when they don't come back at all, you know it's about more than food." —Cesar Millan

᧚

Do not forsake your friend.

PROVERBS 27:10

ON DOG DRINKING AND CAT QUAFFING

Anyone who owns both a dog and a cat can attest to the differing mess levels around each one's water bowl. The reason that cats are such tidy drinkers is that they drink differently than dogs.

A dog will dip its tongue into the water like a ladle—and we know what happens when liquid sloshes around in a ladle. Conversely, a cat touches only the surface of its tongue to the water. According to *MIT News*: "The smooth tip of the tongue barely touches the surface of the liquid before the cat draws its tongue back up. As it does so, a column of liquid forms between the moving tongue and the liquid's surface. The cat then closes its mouth, pinching off the top of the column for a nice drink, while keeping its chin dry."

This technique produces "liquid adhesion," meaning that water sticks to the cat's tongue. And the cat draws back its tongue so quickly that inertia (the tendency of the liquid to continue to follow the movement of the tongue) overcomes the gravity that might otherwise pull the water back down toward the bowl—or the floor. Then the cat snaps its mouth shut before the water can overcome the inertia and escape.

The bottom line: Cats are neater drinkers than dogs. But science, not social refinement or better manners, is the reason. And, as dog people like to counter, drinking is about substance, not style.

Did You Know?
The year 1985 marked the time when cats eclipsed dogs as America's most ubiquitous house pets.

My soul thirsts for God, for the living God.

PSALM 42:2

SHELTER RECIDIVISM

Working as a volunteer at her local dog shelter, Michelle Steigmeyer noticed a troubling trend: some dogs would get adopted but then be returned due to misbehavior in their new homes.

Steigmeyer knew that if she could address the "unadoptable" dogs' issues, she could greatly reduce the number of dogs being returned to the shelter. Working with six dog trainers, she successfully trained and re-homed seventeen behavior-challenged dogs—in just the first four months of her efforts. Soon, she took her initiative national. She purchased a training facility in Indiana and (at press time) had ten other trainers to work with so-called "unadoptable" rescue dogs so that they would be more likely to stay with their families once adopted.

She also launched a website called adoptatraineddog.com,

which showcases the fruits of her efforts with her canine clients. Steigmeyer hopes to expand her efforts with shelters and rescue operations so that dogs will find—and keep—forever homes. For more information, visit adoptatraineddog.com.

Speaking of Dogs . . .

"The poor dog, in life the firmest friend,
The first to welcome, foremost to defend."

John Cab Hobhouse

*(These words are sometimes incorrectly attributed
to Hobhouse's friend Lord Byron.)*

👓

"In my distress I called to the LORD;
I called out to my God. From his temple
he heard my voice; my cry came to his ears."

2 SAMUEL 22:7

77

NO HOT DOGS

It's a sad sight for any dog lover to see: a dog left alone in a car on a hot day. We've all read stories about a dog dying in a vehicle at a mall parking lot or in front of the grocery store, etc.

So, as a dog lover and concerned citizen, what do you do? Stand by the car and try to comfort the dog? Break the window? Call the police?

If you answered "call the police," you are correct, according to Ontario SPCA investigator Scott Silvia. Silvia notes that parked cars can quickly reach deadly temperatures—even on a cloudy day, even if parked in the shade, and even if a window or two is open a crack. After all, a dog has limited ability to cool itself by sweating, so even a brief time in a hot environment can mean brain damage or death.

This means a dog can be in danger even if he's showing no signs of distress. (A dog's normal body temperature is 102 degrees, and irreparable damage can occur once that temp hits 106 degrees.) It's tempting to break a window when you see a dog in peril, but it's also illegal. You would be harming another's property and can be held liable for damages. There is also the risk of injuring the dog or yourself. The best course of action? Call the police or local animal welfare agency.

If you encounter this scenario, note signs of canine distress or heatstroke, which include excessive panting, drooling, or listlessness. But, as mentioned earlier, a dog can be at risk even if he appears to be fine.

The bottom line, of course, is to avoid even the possibility of putting a pet in peril. "Just one stop at the store" can turn into a series of stops. A quick errand at the post office can turn into a long ordeal. So, when the weather heats up, leave your dog at home and encourage others to do the same. Inform them that the temperature inside a vehicle can be up to forty degrees hotter than the outside temperature!

Did You Know?

Dogs have fewer sweat glands than humans, and most of the sweat glands they do have are located on the pads of their paws. A dog's tongue does not have sweat glands, contrary to a popular myth. Panting helps dogs beat the heat when air passes over the saliva-moistened surface of its mouth and tongue.

👓

Apply your heart to instruction
and your ears to words of knowledge.

PROVERBS 23:12

78

WHEN A PICNIC IS NO PICNIC

Who would host a picnic or barbecue without inviting a dog—or six? Dogs love an outdoor shindig, especially all of the inevitable leftovers (which, for a dog, includes that burger you left unattended for a few seconds too long).

So, it might surprise even the most experienced dog owners that summer barbecue/picnic season is also prime pet ER season. For example, veterinarian Dr. Heather Loesner notes that her number one summer surgery is removing corncobs from canine intestinal tracts. Peach-pit removal ranks a close second.

That's why the human diners need to be vigilant and keep a dog entertained and well-fed with safe and proper treats.

Stuffing a toy with a pup's favorite treat and placing it away from the serving and dining area is a great idea. It's also important to clean up scraps quickly and secure them. An overflowing trash can is a buffet table for many dogs. Use a tight-fitting lid—and bungee cords if necessary.

If you fear that a dog has swallowed a peach pit or corn cob, induce vomiting with hydrogen peroxide. Call a vet or emergency hotline if you don't know the proper dose for your pet.

Did You Know?

Contrary to popular belief, eating raw meat or eggs is not a good idea for pet dogs. These foods contain bacteria such as Salmonella and E. coli, which can be as harmful to pets as they are to humans. Further, raw eggs contain an enzyme called avidin, which decreases absorption of the B vitamin biotin, leading to skin and coat problems.

Better a patient person than a warrior,
one with self-control than one who takes a city.

PROVERBS 16:32

79

DOG OLYMPICS

Dog lovers know that border collies are expert sheep dogs, but which border collie is boss?

Dog owners can test their pets' mettle at competitions like the Kingston Sheep Dog Trials Festival, held annually in Kingston, Ontario. Here, nearly seven hundred sheep present a woolly test to dogs over four days of qualifying trials, all leading up to the finals, featuring the top seventeen dogs.

Here's what the competition looks like: Each dog and owner are given a post for their nine minutes of potential glory. Dogs are sent to the left or right to pick up four sheep (two hundred and fifty yards away) and return them to their handler. Next, the dog drives its sheep around a course of gates before penning them and dividing them into two groups. The smoothest, swiftest, and most efficient dogs move on to the finals.

In the finals, dogs work with two groups of ten sheep, and, at one point, they must separate five sheep wearing collars from their fifteen collarless comrades. Sound tough? Well, border collies are one of the world's smartest breeds.

The Kingston event also features demonstrations by K9 police dogs, sheep-shearing showcases, a doggie play zone, and, of course, lots of food trucks for dogs and humans.

Did You Know?

In the mid-1800s, the strongest and bravest of the Cheyenne warriors were known as "Dog Men" because they were seen as the watchdogs of their tribe and its territory.

⌒

And this is love: that we walk in obedience
to his commands. As you have heard from the beginning,
his command is that you walk in love.

2 JOHN 1:6

GRATEFUL AT GROUND ZERO

For 9/11 first responders like the NYPD's Peter Davis, dogs were a lifesaver—in every sense of the word. Davis and his canine partner, a German shepherd named Apollo, worked grueling sixteen-hour days at Ground Zero, rescuing the injured and searching for survivors.

Apollo was one of three hundred and fifty search and rescue (SAR) dogs called to the scene, and, according to an Animal Planet report, "It became evident that the SAR dogs were nearly as distraught as their owners when there were so few survivors to be found."

SAR dogs, who work hand-in-paw with their owners, provide much-needed expertise in a variety of emergencies. They can find a child lost in the wilderness, a skier buried in an avalanche, victims trapped in a collapsed building, or an Alzheimer's patient who has wandered away from home.

For more information on Apollo, as well as Nikie the golden retriever and other brave canines who served after 9/11, watch the Animal Planet documentary *Hero Dogs of 9/11*.

Did You Know?

After the attacks on September 11, blind World Trade Center employee Michael Hingson was led to safety by his guide dog, a Labrador retriever named Roselle.

☙

Your righteousness is like the highest mountains,
your justice like the great deep.
You, LORD, preserve both people and animals.

PSALM 36:6

81

A DOG-LIKE CAT?

This book has addressed the friendly rivalry between dog lovers and cat lovers. Of course, most animal lovers adore both the canine and the feline. But many cat owners sometimes wonder, *Why can't my cat be more like a dog?*

If you've ever echoed this sentiment, consider the Birman cat, perhaps the world's most dog-like cat. Legend has it that

Birmans are descended from the sacred temple cats of Burma. (Another theory is that they are a simple cross-breed of the Siamese and the Longhair.) Whatever the case, Birmans are agreeable cats with long and silky coats, marked by their distinctive white "gloves" (paws). They are clever and not as demanding or vocal as a Siamese or Burmese.

Birmans are friendly, outgoing, and even-tempered. They adapt well to change—a rare trait for cats, who love routine and predictability. Birmans will come to you when called and might even bound to the doorway to greet you after a long day at work, just as a dog would.

So, the next time someone says to you, "Why can't cats be more like dogs?" think of the Birman and answer, "They can."

Conversely, are there dog breeds that are *cat-like*? Indeed. Consider the Shiba Inu, a small Japanese breed. Shibas are affectionate with their people but shy around strangers. They bark very little and even groom themselves like a cat. The Basenji is another dog who rarely barks (although they are known to yodel occasionally). A Basenji is likely to attach to a single human and be very reserved around strangers.

Speaking of Dogs and Cats . . .

"I care not much for a man's religion on whose dog and cat are not the better for it."
Abraham Lincoln

A true friend is always loyal.
PROVERBS 17:17 TLB

82

FIT TO BE CANINE

Some dogs are known for their sleeping and chilling, but almost all canines enjoy (and need) exercise and play as well. However, when picking out a toy to entertain or exercise your dog, choose one best suited for her personality. If your dog is timid, select a toy that is simple and easy to "conquer." (For example, if a gizmo has a too-big "target toy" on its end, it will look like an intimidating opponent, not a fun item of "prey" or play.) If your pup is confident and athletic, you can choose something more challenging.

Try to make interactive play a regular part of your week. Don't play one day, then take a two-week break. Your dog needs consistency. Make a playdate once or twice a day. You need only about fifteen minutes per session but will be surprised what a few minutes of playtime and fun can do for your pet's emotional and physical health—and yours as well.

When playing with your dog, make sure you have all the right moves. Don't wave a toy around frantically. That's not how a canid would hunt in the wild, which requires a combination of stealth and strike. Move the toy like prey, alternating between fast and slow movement. Let your dog plan her moves and carry them out!

Here's another tip: Movements that go away from or across your dog's field of vision will trigger that predator or chase drive. Don't simply dangle a toy in its face, or "attack" with it. Hunting is a mental and physical task, so strive to make your canine playtime confidence building, trust building, and stress relieving. Your dog must have some successful "captures" or she will get frustrated.

Options abound for dog-ercize. If you're a techie, check out games like iTunes' "Game for Dogs" and "Lonely Dog Toy." However, if you and your dog are low-tech, there's probably no beating an old tennis ball or flying disc. Outdoors, a walk, run, or romp on challenging terrain is a great way to build a canine's strength and balance (and a human's too). Play hide-and-seek or chase, or even invent a game of your own. Let your pup play with other dogs if she's well socialized, but be careful of rough and rowdy dogs, especially large ones that could injure your friend.

If you are not into games, take heart. Simple hiking and walking are wonderful activities for your dog. After all, this is what she would be doing out in nature.

Did You Know?

While playing Frisbee with your dog is a classic game, a hard plastic disc can damage your dog's teeth and/or mouth tissues. For a safer playtime, opt for a disc made of softer materials. The waterproof and floatable Floppy Disc (softbitefloppydisc.com) is one alternative.

👓

You will again be happy and dance merrily
with the timbrels.

JEREMIAH 31:4 TLB

83

FAST FRIENDS

Most dog lovers know that the greyhound is the fastest of all dogs, sprinting at top speeds of forty-five miles per hour. If you're an aspiring elite sprinter, this is the dog/training partner for you.

However, did you know that a few other breeds are not far behind the fleet greyhound? Salukis can run at a respectable forty-three miles per hour and can best the swift greyhound if the race is long enough. (The Saluki, which dates back to 2500 BCE, was bred in the Middle East to hunt game like gazelles and hares.)

Also among the fastest pets on the block is the whippet, which can reach top speeds of thirty-six miles per hour. Just how fast is that? A whippet can cover the length of two football fields in about twelve seconds, much quicker than even the fastest NFL athlete!

For those who want a dog who travels at a much more moderate pace, consider the basset hound or the bulldog—or any breed known for a large body and stubby legs.

Indeed, there is a dog for almost any pace—and any place.

Did You Know?

While greyhounds are renowned for their speed, they spend a huge chunk of each day napping and chilling. Some of these feats of lounging can be found on YouTube or other sites. Perhaps it takes a lot of time to rest up for the next big sprint?

Keep traveling steadily along his pathway and
in due season he will honor you with every blessing.

PSALM 37:34 TLB

NOW HEAR THIS!

It's no surprise that our dogs hear better than we do, but how much better? There's no simple answer.

First of all, what do we mean by *better*? Dogs hear a much wider range of frequencies than we do; their low-end range is comparable to ours, at 40 hertz to our 20. It's at the high end that dogs display their audacious auditory. We can detect sounds as high as 23 kilohertz (or 23,000 hertz), but dogs can hear up to 45 kilohertz.

Another advantage dogs enjoy is the ability to move their ears in response to sound, which maximizes their auditory ability. Further, many dogs don't have to cup their ears as we do. Breeds like the German shepherd are blessed with ears that are pre-cupped, or curved, for maximum hear-ability. In practical terms, this means that while we can hear someone talking from about one hundred yards away, our dogs can hear the same conversation up to a quarter mile away (more than four times as far). As for a dog *understanding* a conversation, that's another matter.

Did You Know?

Cats can hear even better than dogs. Their dish-shaped ears, with large echo chambers, give them ultrasonic hearing ability. Some cats can detect frequencies as high as 100 kilohertz (though the average is about 65 kilohertz). A dog's range, as noted above, is about 40 hertz to 45 kilohertz. Humans rank a distant third in the auditory department, maxing out at about 20 kilohertz.

God sets out the entire creation as a science classroom,
using birds and beasts to teach wisdom.

JOB 35:11 MSG

85

CATNIP FOR DOGS?

It makes your cat dance, purr, and tumble, but did you know that catnip (also known as catmint) has many benefits for dogs too?

While catnip is a stimulant for most cats, it's also a canine calm-me-down. Many dog lovers note catnip's powers as a sedative or nerve tonic, and it helps with other issues as well. In addition to helping with tummy troubles like gas or cramping, catnip oil can soothe cuts, scrapes, and scratches. So, consider sprinkling a few fresh catnip leaves in your dog's drinking water, mixing a half-teaspoon or so into dog food, or applying the plant's oil on minor nicks. Of course, check with your vet first. And, when considering catnip, don't stop with your canine.

According to websites like herbwisdom.com and organicfacts. net, catnip can nip a variety of human digestive problems—from indigestion to diarrhea to gas—in the bud. It even helps ease menstrual cramps. Catnip infusions and baths are believed to soothe achy muscles, especially those caused by flu or other illness. For many years, catnip's anti-inflammatory properties have made it a popular treatment for arthritis, hemorrhoids, and bug bites. And a mild catnip tea might alleviate morning sickness, provide a good night's sleep, and calm frazzled nerves. Further, catnip can repel certain insects, making it a popular ingredient in some homemade bug repellants.

To find out how a catnip tea, tincture, or bath balm might help *you*, visit your local natural foods store, or visit websites like wellnessmama.com, herbwisdom.com, organicfacts.net, and webmd.com.

Did You Know?

The herb anise affects dogs the way catnip affects cats. A bit of anise oil can make a dog long on energy and short on common sense. In some greyhound races, the fake rabbit used to urge the dogs to run is anise scented.

A cheerful heart is good medicine.

PROVERBS 17:22

86

TO YOU, BOO!

We all know that Internet fame can be fleeting, but search for "the most popular dog on the Internet," and you will most likely find Boo, the ten-year-old Teddy Bear Pomeranian who has ruled Facebook, YouTube, and other sites for more than seven years. At press time, the diminutive dog had amassed 17.5 million Facebook "Likes" and was featured in four books. He also has his own plush toy and is the "spokes-dog" for the airline Virgin America.

Boo had a modest Facebook page back in 2009, but things blew up for him when pop star (and noted animal lover) Keisha sang the dog's praises on Twitter. Celebs like Kim Kardashian joined the chorus, and an Internet star was born.

Incidentally, Boo is owned by Irene Ahn, who is an executive at Facebook. Cynics have cited this relationship as the secret to Boo's success. But watch one YouTube video starring Boo, and it's clear that this Pomeranian doesn't need any inside help in winning hearts.

Speaking of Dogs . . .

"A dog is grateful for what is, which I am finding to be the soundest kind of wisdom and very good theology."

Carrie Newcomer

👓

Seek good ... that you may live.
Then the Lord God Almighty will be with you.
Amos 5:14

87

COYOTES: A WILEY PET

Ten-year-old Hailey Hanestad has probably never heard of the Flapper-era celebrities Phyllis Gordon and Josephine Baker, but she has something in common with them: a really fast pet. During the height of their fame, Gordon and Baker traveled with cheetahs as pets.

Young Hailey's pet of choice, however, is not quite cheetah-fleet—and it's canine, not feline. Her pet is a "rescue coyote" named Wiley.

Today, of course, times have changed and cheetahs are no longer legal to have as American house pets. Coyotes are banned too, in some states and settings. But if you have a farm, like the Hanestad family of Eau Claire, Wisconsin, you can be on the right side of the law. Especially if the farm includes a large coyote pen, complete with an underground coyote cave.

But, legal or not, is owning a wild animal like a coyote or cheetah a good idea?

It depends on whom you ask. Cheetahs, like coyotes, can be tamed—somewhat. Domestication of these fast cats dates back to 1200 BCE Egypt, when the Egyptians tamed and trained cheetahs to assist them on hunts. More recently, South Africans Hein and Kim Schoeman adopted two cheetah cubs and raised them alongside their two children (ages three and one), recording their experiences in a documentary titled *Cheetah House*. In it, the cheetahs can be seen playing fetch, riding shotgun on car rides, and hanging out with the toddlers. Additionally, cheetahs are legal pets in the United Arab Emirates, in some West Asian countries, and in parts of Africa.

With a technique known as "affection training," cheetahs can be trained to play fetch just like a dog, and to be comfortable around humans. However, the cats have very specific needs. They need to run regularly, with at least two acres of land at their disposal. They require a carefully monitored diet that includes four pounds of meat daily—including the bones.

And even if you can skillfully train and feed your cheetah, you can't expect it to be domesticated like your pet housecat or dog. "Domestication is a process that takes hundreds of generations of domestication breeding," notes Dr. Laurie Marker, a conservation biologist who founded the Cheetah Conservation Fund.

On a similar note, if you peruse "coyote as pets" message boards, you regularly encounter words like "unpredictable," "un-potty-trainable," and "aggressive" (also, "bites!"). Indeed, many of the photos of the Hanestad family and Wiley are charming, but others, including the one where Wiley seems poised to take a huge bite out of the family dog, are frightening.

Veterinarian Chris Bern notes that coyotes and even coyote-dog hybrids "pose a significant risk to the owners and pets or people around them." Besides, if your pet coyote escapes, it can run up to forty-five miles per hour. Good luck catching it!

So, if you are considering a pet coyote, the best advice might be, "Not so fast."

Did You Know?
The word *coyote* is a Spanish derivation meaning "trickster."

෯

Be sure that everything is done properly
in a good and orderly way.

1 CORINTHIANS 14:40 TLB

88

A COP NAMED SEMPER

Imagine joining the police force at just five months of age. That's what happened to Semper, a new employee of the Olympia (Washington) Police Department.

Semper is the protégé of an expert dog handler named Madison Sola Del Vigo, who began working with the pup when he was just nine weeks old. Del Vigo also works in the police department's records center, and her husband, Javier, is a foot-patrol officer.

Unlike his "dad," Semper will not chase down any law breakers. He is in training to be a therapy dog, a role in which he will comfort and assist crime victims during interviews and other difficult scenarios. "Semper's role will be to help victims feel comfortable, help them deal with stress," Lieutenant Paul Lower, a police department spokesman, told *The Olympian* newspaper.

Semper's training regimen requires that he and Del Vigo awaken at six o'clock every morning (appropriate for a dog whose name was inspired by the Marine motto, *Semper fidelis*). The duo works on focus exercises and obedience training. She says she strives to make the process fun and positive. "Semper is motivated to work with me. He's motivated to have fun with me," she says.

She adds that Semper has been a huge morale boost to the entire police force. Lieutenant Lower agrees, saying, "He's been a ball of fun around our department."

Speaking of Dogs . . .

"A hound will die for you but never lie to you."
George R. R. Martin

☍

Cause me to understand the way of your precepts,
that I may meditate on your wonderful deeds.

PSALM 119:27

89

SO HARD TO SAY GOODBYE

Typically, a dog lives about ten years, varying by breed. A boxer's life expectancy is about nine years, while a Samoyed averages twelve years. Miniature poodles typically reach age fourteen.

The oldest dog on record is Maggie the Kelpie, an Australian canine who passed away in 2016 at age thirty—the equivalent of a human reaching two hundred years old. (The oldest cat on record was Crème Puff, from Austin, Texas, who passed away three days after her thirty-eighth birthday. That's like a human living to the age of 182.)

Whenever it happens, saying goodbye to a beloved pet is heart-wrenching. In a survey of 1,300 dog and cat lovers, researchers found that half said losing their canine or feline was as heartbreaking as losing a close relative like an aunt, uncle, or grandparent. A third went even further, comparing a pet death to the death of a parent, sibling, or spouse.

Pet lovers also noted that they mourn their pets for years. More than half of respondents said that their grief for their cat or dog "never goes away."

Writer Amy Sedaris spoke for many pet lovers when she said, "Sometimes losing a pet is more painful than losing a human because in the case of the pet, you were not pretending to love it."

Speaking of Pets . . .

"If there is a heaven, it's certain our animals are to be there. Their lives become so interwoven with our own that it would take more than an archangel to detangle them."

Pam Brown

Blessed are those who mourn,
for they will be comforted.

MATTHEW 5:4

90

THE RIGHT PEDIGREE

The microblogging platform/social networking site Tumblr recently ran a meme that reflects the breed-centric tendencies (or lack thereof) of dog and cat people:

Dog person: "We have a purebred border collie with a Bernese twist."

Cat person: "This is Rita. We love her. She's orange."

However, today's cat owners are becoming more informed about pedigreed cats and how they can be wonderful pets, in the right home. These are lessons that dog lovers have known for a long time.

For example, if you live in an apartment or condo and your lifestyle doesn't allow for lots of exercise, a French bulldog might be the perfect pet. Frenchies are happy with one short daily walk, and if this isn't possible, they will adapt and engage in a bit of indoor playtime. If these bulldogs are walked outside, it should be done in cool weather, as they are very sensitive to heatstroke. (For this reason, they should never be car passengers on a hot day.)

Similarly, the Cavalier King spaniel is the quintessential lap dog, willing to adapt its activity level to yours. Here is a dog that is happy to play, or not. On the other hand, the Gordon setter is a high-energy dog that thrives on vigorous exercise—and gets a bit stir-crazy without it. "A Gordon is a lap dog—for about two minutes," explains T. J. Hafer. "Then it's time to go chase a rabbit across a field."

For families with young children, beagles are a great choice.

They are smart, friendly, happy, and calm. A beagle is small enough to be carried but sturdy enough for energetic play. These dogs love games, and the kids will probably tire out before the beagle does.

For more information on a breed that might be a perfect fit for your home, talk with a veterinarian or research specific breeds on the Internet.

Did You Know?

The wire fox terrier, famous for being spry, agile, and cheerful, has won the Westminster Kennel Club Best in Show award fourteen times—more than any other breed.

૭૩

"Ask, and you will be given what you ask for.
Seek, and you will find. Knock,
and the door will be opened."

MATTHEW 7:7 TLB

91

LOST AND FOUND

According to the ASPCA, 15 percent of pet owners have had a cat or dog go missing.

However, while 93 percent of lost dogs are recovered, the percentage drops to 74 for cats. Further, ASPCA research indicates that while 80 percent of pet owners say it is important to place I.D. tags on their pets, only 30 percent actually provide them. "Overall use of collar I.D. tags is lower for cats than dogs," explains Dr. Emily Weiss, vice president of ASPCA shelter research and development. "The likelihood of your being reunited is lower if it's a cat. People wait longer to look, and about 25 percent don't come home."

If California-based cartoonist Matthew Inman has his way, every housecat will sport an orange collar emblazoned with its name and phone number. That way, if a cat gets loose or lost, the collar will be a signal, shouting, "Help me!" Inman has dubbed his collar campaign the Kitty Convict Project. Its goal is to increase the percentage of missing cats reunited with their owners.

As Inman notes, when dogs are loose, they are often picked up on the assumption that they are lost. When people see a roaming cat, they often assume it is allowed to explore or that it's feral. Inman thinks he can change things. He says he's already sold thousands of his orange Kitty Convict collars (they are available on Amazon.com). The collars are custom-stitched with the cat's name and a contact phone number. "We want to change what people see when they see a cat," he says.

Another new technology that is helping dog and cat lovers keep better track of their pets is Pod. Pod is a small, lightweight real-time GPS tracker that attaches to a dog or cat collar and enables you to locate your pet on-demand. You can also monitor daily activity and even record a pet's personal adventures. For more information, visit podtrackers.com.

Did You Know?
According to the Humane Society, 20 percent of American family dogs have been adopted from animal shelters.

The LORD will rescue his servants;
no one who takes refuge in him will be condemned.

PSALM 34:22

92

TALK TO THE TAIL!

Surveys reveal that more than 95 percent of us talk to our pets. But how many of us listen? Or watch? It's important to pay attention to everything, because, like humans, dogs convey much with nonverbal communication.

For example, if your dog is feeling relaxed and chilled-out, its tail will be lowered and relaxed. The head will be high, with the ears up and the mouth slightly open. A dog who is on alert will have the ears forward, eyes open wide, and mouth closed. The tail will be horizontal, perhaps wagging ever so slightly, like a tree branch on a breezy day.

A dog who is feeling dominant and aggressive will elevate its bristling tail. Its stance will be stiff, with the lips curled and the hackles raised. And a canine who is both fearful *and* aggressive will tuck its tail. The hackles will be raised, with the ears pulled back and the nose wrinkled. A dog in this mode will also lower its head, but that doesn't mean it's cowering.

More than 67 percent of pet owners claim they can understand what their pets are telling them, but we can all improve our communication skills, right?

Did You Know?

Having trouble with your male dog marking his territory in your home—or just struggling with house-training? Companies like Oscar Newman make bellybands that prevent accidents, and they are soft, washable, and won't irritate a dog's skin or fur.

6∂

He performs signs and wonders
in the heavens and on the earth.
DANIEL 6:27

93

ONE FOR THE SHOW?

Even those who are not dog people know about the Westminster Kennel Club's annual dog competition. The first show, held in 1877 when Rutherford B. Hayes was president of the

United States, drew more than 1,200 dogs and proved so popular that an extra day was added to the schedule. Some of the event's proceeds were donated to the ASPCA so the organization could create a home for stray and disabled dogs.

Today, more than 2.5 million people watch the nationally televised event, which is the country's second-longest-running sporting event (just two years behind the Kentucky Derby). More than three thousand canines compete.

The 2017 event will be broadcast by Fox Sports in February (the show has been telecast since 1948). It's appropriate that a sports network is handling the coverage, since some of the dogs train for up to three years for their big moment at Madison Square Garden. According to veteran handler Valerie Nunes-Atkinson, a top dog handler is "part Dr. Doolittle and part Dr. Phil." Nunes-Atkinson, the daughter of a dog breeder, has been practicing her craft since age seven.

When it comes to the coveted Best in Show (BIS) award, the wire fox terrier has been head and paws above the competition, winning fourteen times. At number two on the list is another dog from the terrier group, the Scottish terrier. This short-legged canine, with its classy beard and bushy eyebrows, has amassed eight wins. A smooth fox terrier named Warren Remedy won the first BIS (in 1907), and he went on to win two more top honors. No other dog has matched Champion Warren's feat.

Did You Know?

The WKC show pre-dates the invention of the light bulb, the first automobile, and the invention of basketball.

68

You gave me life and showed me kindness,
and in your providence watched over my spirit.

JOB 10:12

94

AN ORIOLE WHO LOVES DOGS

As an all-star baseball catcher, Matt Wieters knows how to protect home plate. He also knows a lot about protecting animals.

Wieters and his family are the loving owners of Millie, a German shepherd, and two cats—all rescue animals. But the family's efforts go far beyond their home. Wieters is part of Pawject Runway, a canine/feline fashion show held in Baltimore. He has even been known to escort the contestants down the runway. Proceeds go toward animal rescue.

He has also been featured in anti-animal-abuse ads, and is a driving force behind the annual Baltimore Orioles Pet Calendar (the 2017 edition went on sale in August 2016). The calendar features Orioles stars and their pets, including Wieters and Millie. Proceeds from calendar sales go to Baltimore Animal Rescue and Care Shelter, where Wieters' wife, Maria, serves on the board of directors. In recent years, the calendar has raised tens of thousands of dollars for the shelter.

As you read this, the Wieterses' dog and two cats are learning to make room for an even larger family. Maria gave birth to a baby boy, Micah, just before this book went to press.

Did You Know?

The average American household spends more than $1,000 dollars annually on its pet(s). That's more than the amount spent on alcohol, men's clothing, or landline telephones. Incidentally, first-year costs for a large-breed dog average $1,800 ($1,300 for small breeds).

👓

> "You are welcome to stay at my house.
> Let me give you anything you need."
>
> JUDGES 19:20 NCV

A HUSKY ASSISTANT

Morgan Lee Alain is a single young woman who travels the world for her work as a photographer and environmentalist. It's a good thing this twenty-something has a husky assistant. Husky, as in Luna, her beautiful yet formidable companion.

"Luna normally goes in front of me, wanting to know what's ahead," Alain says. "Luna and I have trekked the Canadian

Rockies many times. One particular hike, we were tested by the elements for four days, and our challenges involved extreme cold and steep rugged climbing. Luna overcame all the obstacles with determination and courage."

At home, Luna likes to display her softer side. She is "every child's teddy bear come to life," according to Alain. "It's hard to describe how much joy she brings to my heart." Luna's hobbies include swimming, playing tug-of-war, going for long walks, and eating bugs.

To experience the adventures of Alain and Luna, check out the website morganleealain.com or follow her on Instagram at @morganleealain.

Speaking of Dogs . . .
"There is nothing truer in this world
than the love of a good dog."
Mira Grant

69

May God give you heaven's dew and earth's richness—
an abundance of grain and new wine.

GENESIS 27:28

96

A BULLY NAMED JIMMY CHOO

Artist Rafael Mantesso will never forget his thirtieth birthday. That was the day his wife left him, clearing their apartment of furniture, photographs, and decorations. He was left with nothing but bare walls and a bull terrier named Jimmy Choo.

To bring some joy back into his apartment, Mantesso began snapping photos of Jimmy Choo, often juxtaposing the photos with whimsical drawings. He posted his work on Instagram, and another canine Internet celebrity was born. Sites like *Buzzfeed* and *Huffington Post* took note. Before long, Mantesso and Choo had amassed more than half a million Instagram followers.

Mantesso created a book titled *A Dog Named Jimmy*, featuring 120 examples of his photography/illustration alchemy. Not surprisingly, he also captured the attention of Sandra Choi, director of Jimmy Choo, the luxury shoe brand that inspired the dog's name. The result was a limited-edition capsule collection that included Mantesso's Choo-art on tote bags, handbag pouches, and iPhone cases. (A video was created for the company's website. Go to us.jimmychoo.com to see it—it's hilarious. As is the dog's official website, jimmythebull.com)

As if all this wasn't enough, Mantesso says that canine Jimmy Choo is helping to change public perception of the "bully breeds," highlighting their loving nature and their loyalty to their people. "When people didn't know Jimmy," Mantesso recalls, "they were afraid of him on the streets. They would cross the street so they would not have to pass him. Now, people cross the street to *touch* him and play with him. He loves it."

Mantesso is now creating a foundation to help shelter dogs, and he hopes to create a cartoon show featuring Jimmy. Reflecting on all that has happened, he marvels: "My wife left me with nothing but our dog, so I started taking fun photos of him. The photos I took of him changed my life forever."

Did You Know?

The Dog Museum in Waco, Texas, is home to a huge collection of more than seven thousand dog-related items. Unusual items in the collection include a rifle with a dog-head stock and an aluminum heater shaped like a Scottie.

👓

We love because he first loved us.

1 JOHN 4:19

97

WHAT'S IN A NAME?

Pet lovers know that naming a dog is no job for amateurs. Finding the perfect name can be a labor of much research, reflection, and debate, because it will fit the dog but also reveal something about the "parent."

Many of us look to celebrities for ideas and trends. Can you match the following celebs to their pets, by name? (Here are a few hints: Lauren Conrad's dog is named for a character in her favorite novel. Chloe Grace Moretz's dog is the namesake of the producer of a recent film. And Arianna Grande has established a pattern in naming her pets.)

Vanessa Hudgens	Bronco
Tim Tebow	Atticus
Amanda Seyfried	Darla
Jennifer Lawrence	Elvis
Kate Upton	Fuller
Stephen King	Molly
Arianna Grande	Harley
Chloe Grace Moretz	Sirius Black
Nick Jonas	Pippa
Lauren Conrad	Finn
Jake Gyllenhaal	Fitz

Did You Know?

Seventy percent of Americans include their pets' names on their greeting cards.

🕶

"Blessed are the peacemakers,
for they will be called children of God."

MATTHEW 5:9

Vanessa Hudgens = Darla
Tim Tebow = Bronco
Amanda Seyfried = Finn
Jennifer Lawrence = Pippa
Kate Upton = Harley
Stephen King = Molly

Ariana Grande = Sirius Black
Chloe Grace Moretz = Fuller
Nick Jonas = Elvis
Lauren Conrad = Fitz (for F. Scott Fitzgerald)
Jake Gyllenhaal = Atticus

Hot Names Here!

Here are ten top-trending dog names (in alpha order), according to Barkpost.com:

Annalise
Boo
Burrito
Charlotte
Marnie
Matcha
Pinot
Saint
Shonda
Toast

98

TO TRAIN THE BRAIN

H. J. Springston once said of his pet Tony, "My dog is the smartest, dumbest dog in the world." Many of us can relate to this statement. What can one say about a dog who is following a complex set of instructions one moment and eating out of the cat's litter box the next?

However, savvy dog people know that a bit of patience and perceptiveness can go a long way in enhancing a dog's reasoning powers and trainability. For example, a rescue dog often requires a bit of remedial training to help him learn to stay off the furniture or navigate a new environment.

And did you know that dogs who become deaf (or are born that way) can be trained? Because dogs learn and communicate primarily via observation and body language, a deaf canine can be trained with hand signals rather than voice commands. Many dog lovers use American Sign Language (ASL) to communicate with their pets. In fact, ASL is sometimes used with dogs who can hear just fine, because of its clear commands, like Look, Stop, Leave it, and Down.

Of course, training is easier if you own a super-intelligent breed like the border collie. Rico the border collie was the subject of intense study by psychologist Julie Fischer. He developed a vocabulary of more than two hundred words, a repertoire comparable to that of a three-year-old human, and could perform feats such as selecting a new toy from a batch of familiar playthings, even if the new toy was referred to by a name unfamiliar to him.

Did You Know?

Dogs develop age-related memory problems, just like humans. You can keep your dog alert with puzzles like those developed by Kong and other manufacturers. There are also memory-improving medications available. Consult a veterinarian or dog trainer for more information.

So look me in the eye and show kindness,
give your servant the strength to go on.

PSALM 86:16 MSG

99

A WEIGHTY PROBLEM

Feeding our dogs is the most basic yet most effective way to keep them healthy and show them we care. But do we care too much? According to *The Complete Dog Bible*, almost 40 percent of American dogs are overweight. However, a Purina study indicated that about half the people with overweight dogs did not believe those dogs had a weight problem. This combination of too many calories and too little exercise is leading to canine obesity and its attendant problems: heart disease, arthritis, joint pain and stiffness, and digestive issues.

Several years ago, Purina announced the results of a fourteen-year study in which two groups of Labrador retrievers received nutritionally balanced diets, with one key difference. One group received 25 percent less of the healthy meals. The dogs who ate less lived an average of two years longer than their counterparts. The study's results are particularly revealing, because, just like people, many dogs will overeat if given the opportunity. This behavior is probably rooted in those ancient and wild canine ancestors, who gorged themselves because they knew they might not eat again for days.*

Meal time and snack times are wonderful opportunities to show love to a dog. Follow portion guidelines on dog food packaging, or follow your vet's advice. (Many vets believe that some dogs might not need as much food as the label recommends.) Also keep in mind that no more than 10 percent of a dog's daily calories should come from treats and snacks, whether from a package or *your* dinner plate. (By the way, nearly 80 percent of pet lovers feed their "kids" from their plates.)

Helping your dog achieve and maintain a healthy weight doesn't have to be complicated or difficult. It's as simple as good food, good exercise, and good expert advice.

Did You Know?

Like so many other daily duties, feeding the dog has gone high-tech. Companies like AOS Technologies and Petnet have created remote-control pet feeders. These products allow a dog lover to issue feeder commands via smartphone. Even if you're miles from home, you can give your pup a meal or a snack, using a signal (such as music) to let her know it's feeding time. Some of these feeders include a built-in camera, just in case you want to monitor food consumption or table manners.

---

*   For more information on the study, visit proplan.com.

They are dogs with mighty appetites;
they never have enough.

ISAIAH 56:11

TONGUE TIED

Ask anyone to name a dog's best physical characteristic, and it's unlikely that "tongue" will come out of their mouths.

But a dog's tongue is a thing of wonder. It has more responsibilities than just about any other part, except for the brain. With his tongue, a dog communicates, regulates his temperature, notes tastes and textures, shows affection, consumes food and water, comforts his people, and treats wounds. To achieve all of this, a canine tongue is equipped with eight pairs of muscles and five pairs of cranial nerves (these nerves come directly from the brain via tiny openings in the dog's cranium).

Because a dog's tongue (and teeth too) are so important, many dog lovers make dental care and monitoring part of their regular duties. Brushing teeth and/or using "dental biscuits" or tartar-removing chew toys is one way. So are regular veterinary check-ups. (According to a recent *USA Today* poll, three-fourths of dog owners take their dogs to the vet at least once a year, compared to half of cat owners.)

Of course, you might have heard a dog owner say, "Dogs don't get cavities." This is (mostly) true. However, dogs do get gum disease and infections, which can result in serious health hazards, including heart or kidney damage.

Did You Know?

Imagine the ordeal of brushing the teeth of Zorba, the largest dog on record. The English mastiff weighed 343 pounds and measured 8 feet 3 inches from his nose to his tail.

👓

No human being
can tame the tongue.

JAMES 3:8

101

SAINT DOG

Many people think dogs are saints. Some truly are. The Saint Bernard breed was developed in the 1600s by Swiss monks at the Hospice of Saint Bernard, which was a refuge for travelers crossing mountain passes between Switzerland and Italy.

Descended from the mighty Roman mastiffs, the Saint Bernards plowed paths through the snow, guarded people, and served as search and rescue dogs. During a two-hundred-year-period,

• •

these dogs saved more than two thousand lives, aiding everyone from lost children to Napoleon's soldiers.

With their keen sense of smell, Saint Bernards could find the lost and the injured, even if they were buried in snow. The dogs often worked in groups of two or three, with one dog staying with the rescued person and the other(s) bounding off to bring help. Often, a Saint Bernard would lie atop a freezing victim, keeping him or her warm until aid arrived. And, yes, there are legends of the dogs being equipped with casks of brandy to warm a person in peril, but there is no documentation to support this practice.

With apologies to Beethoven and Cujo, the patron saint of all Saint Bernards is probably Barry, who lived at the Hospice of Saint Bernard in the early 1800s. During his time there, he saved the lives of at least forty people (some sources put the number at more than one hundred). One of these was a half-frozen boy whom Barry somehow loaded onto his broad back and carried to safety.

As tales of Barry's heroics spread through Switzerland, the locals began calling Saint Bernards "Barryhunds" in his honor.

Today, a likeness of Barry (1800–1814) stands in the Natural History Museum in Bern, Switzerland.

Did You Know?
Saint Bernards are named for Great Saint Bernard Pass, home to the hospice where they were bred, and where they served so faithfully. The pass itself is the namesake of Saint Bernard of Clairvaux (1090–1153), a French abbot and reformer.

Rescue me from my enemies, LORD,
for I hide myself in you.
PSALM 143:9

About the Authors

Todd Hafer

Hello, my name is Kaycee, and I am Todd Hafer's rescue Gordon setter. I cannot comment on his writing ability as I am not a big reader, but he is a good running companion. He is slowing down, but given the fact that he's like 350 in dog years, it's not surprising.

He takes me on car rides, which I love (unless the destination is the vet, with her evil nose drops). And he once plunged into San Francisco Bay, in December, to save me this one time when I planned to swim after a duck. (Turns out I can't swim.)

So I think I will keep him, even though he did write *101 Amazing Things about Cat Lovers* before writing this book. But seriously, enough with the nose drops already.

Jedd Hafer

Jedd Hafer's canines, Theodore and Dwayne, would like you to know that Jedd loves dogs and food (but not dog food). He is a national speaker for the Love and Logic Institute, Inc. Working with kids in trouble for the past twenty-one years, he has contributed to *Men's Health* and Lifetime Television's *Teen Trouble* with Josh Shipp. Jedd is a father of four kids (who are sometimes trouble) and has written many books with his brother Todd.

For more information on Jedd and Todd Hafer,
follow them on Facebook or visit their website, haferbrothers.com.

Partial Bibliography

Bryson, Bill. *One Summer: America 1927*. New York: Anchor Books, 2013.

Hafer, Todd. *Everything Romance: A Celebration of Love for Couples*. Colorado Springs: WaterBrook Press, 2011.

Hafer, Todd. *Fun Facts for Hunters*. Uhrichsville, Ohio: Barbour & Company, 2010.

Hafer, Todd. *101 Amazing Things About Cat Lovers*. Racine, Wisconsin: BroadStreet Publishing Group, LLC, 2016.

Mehus-Roe, Kristin. *The Original Dog Bible*. Irvine: BowTie Press, 2009.

Moderndogmagazine.com.

Nicolewilde.com.

Petmd.com.

The Register-Guard (Eugene, OR), August 14, 2016.

Traverse City Record Eagle, (Traverse City, MI), February 11, 2016.

White, Ronald C., Jr. *A. Lincoln: A Biography*. New York: Random House, 2009.

Wolfpark.org.